DISCOVERING THE MOVIES

CINÉMATOGRAPHE LUMIÉR

DISCOVERING THE MOVIES

An Illustrated Introduction to the Motion Picture

Cecile Starr

VAN NOSTRAND REINHOLD COMPANY
New York   Cincinnati   Toronto   London   Melbourne

For Suzanne and Marco

A selection of the films described in **Discovering the Movies** has been brought together for convenient 16mm rental and purchase by the publisher. For an up-to-date listing of titles and prices, write VNR Films, Van Nostrand Reinhold Company, 450 West 33rd Street, New York, New York 10001.

Van Nostrand Reinhold Company Regional Offices:
New York   Cincinnati   Chicago   Millbrae   Dallas
Van Nostrand Reinhold Company International Offices:
London   Toronto   Melbourne

Library of Congress Catalog Card Number 71-176078

Type set by V & M Typographical, Inc.
Printed and Bound by Toppan Printing Co., Ltd. **Tokyo, Japan**

Published in 1972 by Van Nostrand Reinhold Company
450 West 33rd Street, New York, N.Y. 10001
Published simultaneously in Canada by
Van Nostrand Reinhold Ltd.

16 15 14 13 12 11 10 9 8 7 6 5 4 3 2 1

Contents

Foreword

Vachel Lindsay in 1916

On the Study of Film

"The invention of the photoplay," poet Vachel Lindsay wrote in his book *The Art of the Moving Picture* in 1915, "is as great a step as was the beginning of picture writing in the stone age." Lindsay's ideas about language and its relation to pictures place him squarely alongside the most modern communications-minded thinkers of today:

> Yesterday we were preeminently a word-civilization. . . . We were led by Patrick Henry, the orator, Benjamin Franklin, the printer. . . . Here then comes the romance of the photoplay. . . . There is many a babe . . . not over four years old who has received more pictures into its eye than it has had words enter its ear. . . . Often the images are violent and unseemly, a chaos of rawness and squirm, but scattered through the experience is a delineation of the world.

Vachel Lindsay lectured on the movies at Columbia University as early as 1916, and later at the Chicago Art Institute. He was the first film critic of *The New Republic* magazine, possibly the first American to sign his name to regular film reviews.

In addition to such well-known poems as "The Congo" and "Abraham Lincoln Walks at Midnight," Vachel Lindsay wrote poems in praise of his favorite movie stars—comparing comedian John Bunny to the jester Yorick, and calling Mae Marsh "madonna in an art/As wild and young as her sweet eyes."

Lindsay saw other values in the moving pictures—the values of reality: "The shoddiest silent drama may contain noble views of the sea." He believed that if a film was worth seeing at all, it was worth seeing at least three times.

Vachel Lindsay also foresaw a time when film would be studied in schools and colleges throughout the country, when scholars and critics would be "learned in the flavors of early moving picture traditions." He saw the movies as an art in their own right, and wrote that the "supreme photoplay" will give us things that have been "but half-expressed" in the other arts.

Those of us who advocate and practice the study of film in schools today are generally considered part of the educational forefront. In a sense we are. But in another sense we are about fifty years behind such visionaries as Vachel Lindsay, who recognized the artistic value and potential of movies even in their earliest, most primitive state.

In the years since Vachel Lindsay wrote *The Art of the Moving Picture*, many colleges and universities have introduced courses and full degree programs in film study and filmmaking. More recently, high schools—and even grade schools—are including film study as a vital addition to their filmmaking programs, or as part of their studies in art, English, drama, and social studies, or occasionally as an independent film course.

Film study can be approached in many ways. This book is based on ways I have found most successful in my own film teaching over the past eighteen years. It urges students and teachers to discover, with their own eyes, the exciting developments in film art and history. It fosters a forward-looking exploration of film history, rather than a backward glance from our own, often jaded, viewpoint.

"The early motion picture traditions" advocated by Vachel Lindsay are stressed here, not because they are old and venerable, but because in my experience the greatest number of students have found them most enjoyable and easiest to learn from.

Discovering the Movies stresses three main types of film—the story film, the reality film, and the fantasy film—and attempts to show how these types have evolved and how they interrelate. It places strong emphasis on the fantasy film as being most essential to a basic understanding of the illusory qualities of the motion picture, while at the same time having special appeal to youngsters, particularly those of pre-teen and early teen ages. This approach stresses the idea that movies are made by people, not by cameras, and that every important film bears the distinguishing characteristics of an individual creative spirit, often working alongside creative collaborators.

Because words are always inadequate in any approach to film, this book includes many illustrative still pictures. But the films themselves must be seen to be really understood. (Specific information about their availability for school or other use is given in the Study Notes at the end of the book.) Only when you have discovered the films for yourself—or, if you are a teacher, only when you have seen your students' reactions to them—can you begin to sense how exciting and rewarding film study can be.

What is a Motion Picture?

Between each of these small rectangles the shutter closes and plunges us into total darkness, only to return us to full light with the next rectangle. . . . I have calculated that if I see a film that lasts an hour, I am in fact plunged for twenty minutes in total darkness.

—Swedish director Ingmar Bergman

There are many kinds of motion pictures—long ones and short ones, silent and sound, black-and-white and color, lively and dull, funny and sad, photographed and drawn—yet all have these elements in common: there must be *pictures,* and the pictures must *move.* To be accurate, I should say that the pictures must seem to move, for what we see on the screen is not real motion but an *illusion* of motion, a kind of modern magic.

We all know that motion pictures are still pictures, printed one after another on strips of film, with each frame or image differing only slightly from those that precede and follow it. We know that when they are whirled through a projector at the proper speed the images seem to move. Yet no matter how well we know this, when we see a movie the illusion is almost always stronger than our awareness of its unreality.

To understand the film medium—its past, its present, and its future possibilities—we will find ourselves referring over and over again to these three essential and interrelated elements: pictures, movement, illusion.

"The screen is an art of the illusion of reality," Welford Beaton observed in his book, *Know Your Movies.* "None of its elements is real. It is composed entirely of shadows, which are real only in the imagination of the beholder."

Beaton reminds us that we imagine with our picturing sense, not in the abstract. And since in our daily lives we have more imaginary joys and sorrows than real ones, it just may be that imagination is the biggest, most important thing in our lives. Certainly without imagination we could make very little sense of the movies.

8mm, Super 8, 16mm, and 35mm film strips (Notice the sound track alongside the 16mm film.)

How the Movies Began

No one man invented moving pictures, which for a long time meant moving drawings. They grew out of scores of accidents and observations, guesses and experiments.
　　　　—Kenneth Macgowan, in *Behind the Screen*

The Greeks, Egyptians, even cavemen, tried to show motion in some of their paintings and sculptures. But it was not until the nineteenth century, when the Industrial Revolution mechanized the wheel and put nearly everything into motion, that the idea of moving pictures began to obsess a number of people.

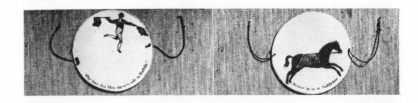

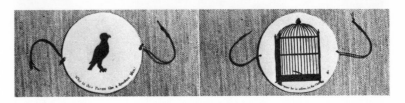

Magic Lanterns, which were first discovered in the sixteenth century, became a popular home entertainment in the nineteenth century. They involved the *projection of enlarged pictures* on a wall or sheet, which could then be viewed at one time by a number of people. Often the pictures were moved back and forth with levers, giving a change of positions rather than a semblance of motion.

The Thaumatrope ("wonder-turning") was a popular toy, but, more importantly, it was scientific evidence of the newly recognized principle of *persistence of vision*. When its strings were pulled taut, the pictures on either side of the disk seemed to blend into a single image: the bird seemed to be inside the cage, the rider seemed to be on the horse, and so on. The Thaumatrope set the vogue for long impressive names taken from Latin or Greek.

Persistence of vision is the phenomenon that causes an image to remain imprinted on the retina of the eye for a fraction of a second after it has passed from view. Thus, when a flashlight is twirled in the dark, we sometimes retain all the images at once and see an entire circle of light at one time.

The study of persistence of vision led to the next important discovery in making pictures move: the drawing of *successive phases of a motion.*

The devices shown on these pages follow one basic pattern: pictures showing successive phases of a motion were painted on a circular device, spun, and viewed in a way that made the images blend into each other, giving the illusion of real motion.

The Phenakistoscope ("deceiving view"), a slotted disk turned and viewed in a mirror, was the first device to show successive stages of a motion and give it lifelike reproduction. It was invented in 1832 by a Belgian physicist named Joseph Plateau, who went blind in the course of his investigation of the persistence of vision.

FRENCH REVOLUTION

The Zoetrope ("wheel of life") separated the pictures from the turning device, so that one apparatus could show many different picture series. It was invented in the 1830s by an English mathematician named William George Horner, and by the 1860s had become a popular household amusement.

The Praxinoscope ("action-view") eliminated the slots and thus provided a steady flow of light and a clearer moving image. It was patented in 1877 by the Frenchman Emile Reynaud.

Reynaud later added backgrounds, a miniature stage, and artificial lighting, and called it the Praxinoscope Theater.

The images might be realistic or fanciful, but in each of these devices only one simple circular motion could be shown over and over again. Repetition as a means of holding the viewer's attention occurs often in later movies. But repetition with no variation and no advancement soon becomes monotony; Reynaud wished to expand his moving-picture-circle into something that would be even more spectacular.

At Reynaud's Théâtre Optique (Optical Theater), a real theater that he operated in Paris from 1892 to 1900, an estimated half-million people came to see what might be called the first animated moving-picture stories. Here Reynaud could project as many as *600 successive pictures in one strip*. Thirty mirrors in the center of the apparatus, combined with lenses and other mirrors, permitted him to show *life-size moving images* on a screen before a *full-size audience*. Reynaud could now depict full incidents, one after another, each with its own emotional values, and each contributing to the development of a little story.

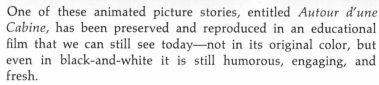

Scenes from Reynaud's *Autour d'une Cabine*, as reproduced in Roger Leenhardt's motion picture, *Animation: The Toy That Grew Up*

One of these animated picture stories, entitled *Autour d'une Cabine*, has been preserved and reproduced in an educational film that we can still see today—not in its original color, but even in black-and-white it is still humorous, engaging, and fresh.

These were only drawings that moved. We can hardly imagine how sensational it was to see photographs move for the first time. It was as exciting to our grandparents and great-grandparents as it would be to us today if we picked up a newspaper and saw the picture on the front page get up and walk around! Unbelievable! But of course, it didn't happen all at once.

Photographs in Motion

As in the development of moving drawings, many people worked for many years to bring together the different elements that formed the basis of what was sometimes called motor photography.

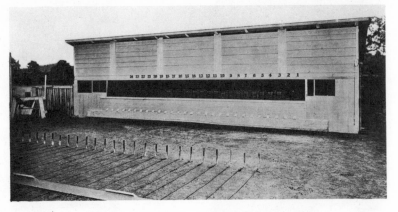

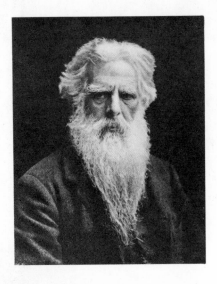

Among the most successful was one who called himself Eadweard Muybridge (his real name was Edward Muggeridge). Muybridge was able to photograph successive phases of a real movement—but he could not do it with one camera. Instead he set up a row of twenty-four still cameras, to take twenty-four action photographs of a galloping horse—allegedly at the request of former California governor Leland Stanford, who had bet that all four feet leave the ground at one point in a horse's gallop.

Many versions of this story have been reported, none of which is known to be true. But it is true that, after a number of attempts, Muybridge was able to photograph the moving horse; in fact, he spent the next twenty years photographing animals and humans in an almost encyclopedic variety of motions. Strips of his "startling, instantaneous photographs" were sold for use in the Zoetrope, for home viewing.

Muybridge also projected the photograph strips, using a machine he called the Zoopraxiscope, which combined the projected image of the Magic Lantern with the picture-disk of the Phenakistoscope.

17

Muybridge's work was seen in France by Dr. E. J. Marey, who had tried many ways of measuring and reproducing motion. Now Marey attempted to reproduce *successive images on a single photographic plate.*

At first, to make as clear a record as possible, Marey dressed his subject in black with a white line running down his arms and legs, and then photographed him against a black background. Marey called his camera the Chronophotographe ("time-light-writing").

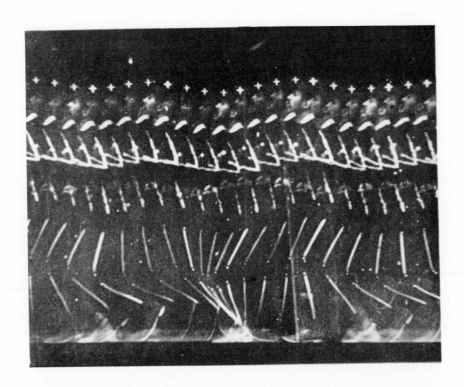

Using George Eastman's newly invented celluloid film strips, Thomas Edison's associates developed the Kinetoscope ("moving-view"), a peep-show machine with a circular strip of photographs that lasted twenty seconds or so. It was shown publicly in 1891. Like the picture strips of the Zoetrope and Praxinoscope, these moving pictures had no beginning, middle, or end.

Pictures of Sandow the Strongman flexing his muscles, or Annie Oakley shooting clay disks, could start and stop at any point. They had no particular meaning, but they did move. They could be viewed by only one person at a time.

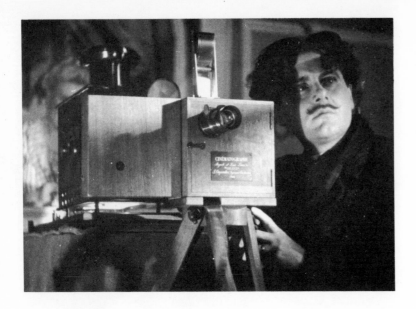

It is generally agreed that the first public showing of projected moving pictures took place in Paris at the end of 1895. It was the work of two scientist-brothers, Louis and Auguste Lumière, who called their camera-projector the Cinématographe ("motion-writing"). Their large-as-life moving pictures of workers leaving the factory, baby at breakfast, and the train arriving in the station show real and complete occurrences.

Although filmed always from a fixed position, in a sense they tell a little story, or part of a story: workers leave the factory, and when they have left the scene is finished; baby eats cereal, smiles, eats more, and that scene is finished; the train pulls into the station, people get off, and that scene is finished.

So great and so lifelike was the enlarged illusion of reality in motion that men and women gasped at the sight of the oncoming train, and some are said to have fainted away.

By 1895, the essential elements of the moving picture had come together: pictures of successive phases of a motion, drawn or photographed on strips of film, projected rapidly one after another in huge enlargement. The constant refining of these elements, with additional effects in color, sound, and occasionally a third dimension, has been the concern of scientists and technicians ever since.

Lewis Jacobs, in the opening paragraph of *The Rise of the American Film*, points out that the motion picture developed through the co-operation of the scientist, the artist, and the businessman. The scientist wants to make pictures move as accurately as possible; the artist wants to make moving pictures express his creative ideas and feelings; the businessman wants to make money. It is the artist's achievements that will mainly concern us in this introduction to the movies. Some film artists have become famous; some are almost unknown. But they have this in common: to some extent they have been free to explore and experiment, to make the films they have wished to make. They are the discoverers of film art. Through their efforts we can begin to discover the movies for ourselves.

The Great Méliès

I was born an artist in my soul, very adroit with my
hands, creative with most materials, inventive, and
a comedian by nature. I was an intellectual and a
manual laborer, at the same time.

—Georges Méliès

22

Since film is a form of magic, it should not surprise you to learn that the first great film artist actually was a magician. His name is Georges Méliès, and he had the good fortune to attend the first performance of the Lumières' Cinématographe show in Paris.

Méliès sensed at once the marvelous possibilities of the moving-picture machine and wanted to buy one—but it was not for sale. But within a few months he had acquired a similar machine from other sources and was filming simple street scenes, along with his own magic tricks performed on stage.

One day Méliès discovered, by accident, that the moving-picture camera could create a new kind of magic all its own.

> Would you like to know how it first came to me to apply trickery to cinema? Quite simply, believe me. A jamming of the camera I used in the beginning (a rudimentary camera, in which the film often got torn or caught and refused to advance) produced an unexpected effect one day when I was photographing prosaically in the Place de l'Opéra; it took a minute to unjam the film and start the camera going again. During this minute, the passers-by, the bus, and carriages had moved on, of course. In projecting the roll of film, joined together at the point where the interruption had taken place, I saw a bus suddenly turned into a hearse, and men changed into women. Trick by substitution (called *truc à arrêt*) was discovered, and two days later I filmed the first metamorphoses of men into women, and the first sudden disappearances which at the beginning had so great a success.

—written by Georges Méliès in 1907

Méliès' had discovered that by interrupting and rearranging the normal pattern of successive phases of a motion, he could make his subject seem to become something else. To Edison's simple repetitions and the Lumières' chronological unfolding, Méliès added a new possibility for film movement: transformations that could change an image, or part of an image, into something entirely different.

Extraordinary Illusions (about 3 minutes, silent)
Produced by Georges Méliès in 1903

Méliès himself appears in the leading role, as he does in nearly
all his films. Aside from the opening shot—a double-exposure
that vibrates disturbingly—*Extraordinary Illusions* is a succession of dazzling effects and delightful humor. Méliès removes
from a seemingly empty box the arms, legs, torso, and head of
a dummy, which he assembles and then transforms (in mid-air)
into a dancer. He sends the empty box offstage by itself, coaxing
it along as though it were able to see and understand him.

Then the transformations begin in earnest: the dancer turns
into a cook, the cook back into the dancer and later into a bag
of rags—with a precision that demands much preparation and
skill. Persistence of vision keeps us from spotting the minor
discrepancies and makes us believe we have seen one image
become something else. Even when you know that two jumps
were made by two different people, and that the two strips of
film were joined together in the middle, the effect in actual
motion is still breathtaking today.

Notice the variety Méliès uses to prevent these fairly similar
transformations from being monotonous—across screen right
to left, down the center, down the right side, moving naturally
and freely in one continuous flow of magical delight, faster
and faster until the film ends.

Extraordinary Illusions is a film I have seen forty or fifty
times and have never found uninteresting. When you watch
it, you have to look carefully, for much of its photographic
quality has been lost in the many years since it was made. In
addition, its magical effects follow one another so rapidly that
if you turn your head or blink your eyes for just a second, you
will miss much of the motion-picture illusion that makes Méliès
a master of filmmaking.

24

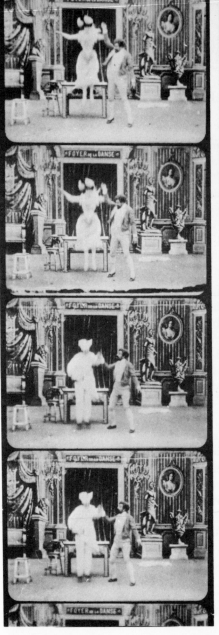

In the years between 1896 and 1913, Georges Méliès made some 500 short films, many of which no longer exist. Their titles—*A Hypnotist at Work* or *The Haunted Castle*—give us an idea of their magical possibilities.

Méliès began putting separate scenes together in the form of a continuing story while the Edison and Lumière programs still were made up of separate unrelated one-minute items. Méliès' film versions of Cinderella, Bluebeard, and many other fairy tales were immediately successful; some lasted as long as five minutes, or longer, with eight or ten or more scenes joined together to tell the whole story.

But with his first science-fiction film, based on a story by Jules Verne, Méliès surpassed all his previous efforts in magic, humor, pacing, storytelling, and splendor.

A Trip to the Moon (about 12 minutes, silent)
Produced by Georges Méliès in 1902

Méliès advertised the film as "Ten Extraordinary and Fantastical
Cinematograph Series in Thirty Scenes," and in his 1903 American catalogue scenes were listed by name:

The scientific congress at the Astronomic Club.

Planning the trip. Appointing the explorers and servants.
Farewell.

The workshops. Constructing the projectile.

The astronomers enter the shell.

Loading the gun.

. . . Fire . . .

The flight through space. Approaching the moon.

Landed right in the eye!!!

Within the limitations of the fixed camera and the stagelike acting area, Méliès made ingenious efforts to create new motion effects:

the spinning earth seen from the moon;

the constellation-ladies drifting through space;

mushrooms growing and moon-men disappearing in puffs of smoke.

You may wonder why such an old-fashioned film is called a work of art. As primitive and as limited as it obviously is, this film is still a marvelous display of the unique talents of one man—his imagination, his personality, his humor, his technical inventiveness, his artistry. Although filmmakers today can do all the tricks Méliès could do, and many more, no one since Méliès has done them with such freshness and skill.

But even in the hands of so creative a person as Méliès, this stage-bound film style has many shortcomings. In the opening shot, for example, when scientists have gathered from all over the world (as their elaborate costumes indicate), they must gesture wildly just to be seen from such a distance.

Many of the scenes are filled to overflowing with people, props, elaborate sets, and odd costumes; the eye cannot take it all in. (Of course, we are seeing the films in rather poor black-and-white prints; originally they were painted by hand in brilliant splashes of color, which emphasized the leading players and actions.)

In all his films, Méliès usually wrote or adapted the story, designed the sets and costumes (in various shades of grey, which photographed better than colors did), hired and rehearsed the performers, played the leading (and sometimes the only) role, directed the filming, developed and printed the exposed film, edited the trick shots, and, when this was done, took the film under his arm and went out to sell it.

Always the showman, Méliès recruited his army of performers from all the theaters and variety halls of Paris, even the Folies-Bergères. His studio in the suburbs of Paris was the first movie studio in the world.

> [Méliès] discovered that film is a new way of seeing, interpreting, and also distorting, reality, in accordance with the creator's will. His technical virtuosity offers the first clues to the working of the cinematic imagination.
> —John Howard Lawson, in *Film: The Creative Process*

Méliès made marvelous discoveries that greatly increased the expressiveness of film language—but although he made everything else move, it seems never to have occurred to him that the camera also could move.

One of his last great films, *Conquest of the Pole*, made in 1912, is largely an elaboration of the techniques used ten years earlier in *A Trip to the Moon*. There are more scenes, and they are shorter, but Méliès saw no need to break them down into smaller bits and details. The airship is more elaborate; more planets and comets float by in space; the Monster at the North Pole is considerably more complex in design and workings than any earlier one (and is possibly the most lovable of all Méliès' fantastic creations). Over the years, Méliès' films had not changed. But it was his misfortune that the movies had.

In the last twenty years of his life, Méliès made no movies. It is said that at a time of despair he burned his prints and negatives (but another story says they were seized during World War I and melted down for their silver content). He was, in either case, almost forgotten until one day late in his life he was discovered selling toys in a small shop inside a railroad station in Paris.

Méliès is often credited as the first person to bring a story pattern to the moving picture, using literary subjects, actors, costumes, and sets, all borrowed from the theater. But, in my opinion, Méliès used story merely as a vehicle for fantasy, and it is his exploration of the fantasy elements of the cinema that gives his films their greatest artistic significance.

"We're all lineal descendents of Georges Méliès," avant-garde filmmaker Hans Richter has written. "He was the first to know what the cinema was for."

Telling a Story in Pictures

You will see that this little clicking contraption with the revolving handle will make a revolution in our life—in the life of writers. It is a direct attack on the old methods of literary art. We shall have to adapt ourselves to the shadowy screen and to the cold machine. A new form of writing will be necessary. I have thought of that and I can feel what is coming.

But I rather like it. This swift change of scene, this blending of emotion and experience—it is much better than the heavy, long-drawn-out kind of writing to which we are accustomed. It is closer to life. In life, too, changes and transitions flash by before our eyes, and emotions of the soul are like a hurricane. The cinema has divined the mystery of motion. And that is its greatness.

—attributed to Leo Tolstoy in an interview
on his eightieth birthday in 1908

The man who first discovered that moving pictures could convey a full range of actions, feelings, and thoughts is the great director, D. W. Griffith. Griffith originated many new techniques, but this is not why he is considered great. His main achievement was his ability, within a few years, to create a new language of moving images, which linked the audience to the screen through the mind and feelings as well as through the eyes.

When David Wark Griffith died in 1948, critic James Agee wrote: "There is not a man working in movies, or a man who cares for them, who does not owe Griffith more than he owes anybody else."

How can an entire art owe so much to one man? To understand the answer, let's first go back for a moment to Méliès' *A Trip to the Moon* and think of it not as fantasy, of which it is a superb example, but as a moving-picture story, exclusively. E. M. Forster tells us in his book, *Aspects of the Novel*, that a simple time sense is the basic element of the story: this happened, and then that happened, and so on. Stories hold our attention, Forster adds, because we all want to know what happens next. This simple time sense exists in *A Trip to the Moon:* first there is the meeting, then the workers build the rocketship, the scientists land on the moon, they are taken prisoner, and finally they return to earth.

But, Forster tells us, often we want to know more; we want to know what the characters feel and think. Here Méliès not only failed to appease our curiosity, but he didn't even try. Simple astonishment or anger may be contained in an actor's frantic gestures, but Méliès attempted no more. Rarely do his characters achieve individuality. What one does, all do. If one stretches and yawns, all stretch and yawn; if one goes to sleep, all go to sleep. Even the chief scientist is lost amid the group of minor scientists, since he is always as far away from us as the others. The very actions of his performers are often those of mechanical toys.

New things begin to happen, however, when a film drama is enacted with some of its scenes out-of-doors. Such a film is *The Great Train Robbery*, released just a year after *A Trip to the Moon*, and based not on a science-fiction story but on a number of real train hold-ups by outlaw bands. It was filmed in New Jersey, which was about as far west as film producers would go in those days.

The Great Train Robbery (about 12 minutes, silent)
Directed by Edwin S. Porter for the Edison Company in 1903

Only five of the fourteen scenes of this film were shot indoors. One is a famous close-up of a bandit firing point-blank into the audience—a shot so startling that it could be used either to open or close the film, the Edison catalogue proclaimed. In another indoor shot, an actual train is shown in motion through an open window.

But in the totally outdoors scenes even more startling techniques emerge. One exciting scene takes place atop a moving locomotive. A new sense of depth is given in the vertical lines of the train tracks, as the robbers force the engineer toward us to uncouple the cars.

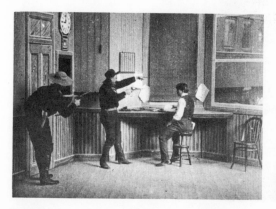

Time also becomes more complex and more real. Some scenes take place simultaneously: the townspeople are on a wild spree in the saloon . . . while the robbers escape with money and valuables. The camera moves somewhat unsteadily to keep the robbers in view as long as possible after they jump from the train and run down the embankment. In unrestricted open spaces, with scenes of fast action, camera movement becomes natural, almost instinctive.

In such scenes as these we feel for the first time that more is happening than we can see, that the action is all around us, not just in front of us, and consequently that the film is *really real*. We begin to have the illusion not only of movement, but of spatial reality as well.

The Great Train Robbery was a sensation in 1903 and for many years afterward. Its director, Edwin S. Porter, had gone to work for the Edison Company in 1891, when he was still in his twenties. Before that he had worked as a telegraph operator, plumber, skating exhibitionist, sign-painter, custom tailor, and electrician in the Navy, according to *The New York Times*. He made his last motion picture in 1915, and at the time of his death in 1941 was almost completely forgotten by the film industry. Many fortunes, including that of the Warner Brothers, it is said, were made by showing *The Great Train Robbery* in the popular Nickelodeon parlors of the time.

Porter's innovations did not lead him to many further discoveries. In *Rescued from an Eagle's Nest* (1907), Porter combined real and artificial outdoors scenes, with incongruous results. Even at the time, the film was not well received. *The Motion Picture World* commented on its poor lighting, its poor blending of the outside photography with the studio work, its too-evident trick of using a fake eagle with wire wings. "We looked for better things," the review concluded.

And better things were coming!

The father who rescues his child from the eagle's nest was an aspiring author and stage actor playing his first role in the movies. Because film work was looked down on by theater people, he used the name Lawrence Griffith.

This was the man destined to discover the language of the dramatic film—David Wark Griffith.

D. W. Griffith: Pictures for the Imagination

If Edwin S. Porter had done little to advance film style in the four years that separated *The Great Train Robbery* and *Rescued from an Eagle's Nest*, what did Griffith do in the next four years that was to change movie history?

He had given up acting, for one thing, and by 1911 had directed about 400 one- and two-reel films for the Biograph Company, averaging two or three productions a week and working an estimated fourteen hours a day, seven days a week.

One of Griffith's most successful short films was *The Lonedale Operator*, a railroad romance-and-rescue thriller made in 1911 and starring Blanche Sweet and Frank Grandin. The heroine and hero are unlike any characters that might have appeared in a Méliès or Porter film; they are alive and real; they feel and think—and we understand and share their feelings and thoughts.

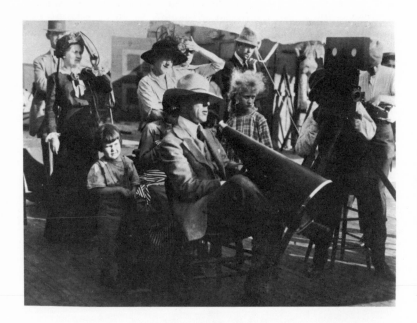

"The task I'm trying to achieve is above all to make you see."

—D. W. Griffith

The Lonedale Operator (about 14 minutes, silent)
Directed by D. W. Griffith; photographed by G. W. Bitzer;
screenplay by Mack Sennett
Produced by the Biograph Company in 1911

Like *The Great Train Robbery*, *The Lonedale Operator* involves
trains, robbers, good guys, and a chase, to which Griffith has
added a love story of unusual subtlety. In style and technique
he has added so much that we can indicate only a few of his
many achievements.

Throughout *The Lonedale Operator*, inside or out, the stage-line
no longer exists. Actors no longer move horizontally across
the screen, exiting and entering from the sides. They move
freely toward us, away from us, diagonally, at any angle.

The fixed-camera scene no longer exists; in its place is the
sequence—a group of shorter shots that, like pieces of a jigsaw
puzzle, contain bits of information that tell us little until they
have been properly put together.

Griffith's camera, in the hands of his gifted operator, G. W.
Bitzer, is placed in the midst of the action; no longer does it
view everything equally and dispassionately from one faraway
fixed position. When an actor registers emotion, the camera is
close enough to show the emotion on the actor's face. A
wrinkled forehead can convey fear more effectively than arms
flung wildly in the air. The close-up had been used before, but
Griffith's close-ups are not used purely for sensation—they are
essential to the development of the story.

Only in the final editing of these close-ups, freer gestures, and the bits and pieces of action can we begin to understand Griffith's growing mastery of the film medium. Take, for example, four quite simple shots, about midway through the film, and see how they relate to each other, and to us, through intercutting of images.

Blanche Sweet stands near the office window and waves (to the left side of the screen)

Frank Grandin, the engineer, leans out of the locomotive window and waves (to the right)

Blanche throws a kiss toward the window

Frank's arm continues waving, getting smaller and smaller as the train moves past the station

What we see in these four shots is partially what the actors might have seen (although the two sets of shots were taken on different days in different places)—not as they could actually have seen it but as the camera can best reveal it. No longer do we witness simple actions; now they have meaning and emotional values. We see Blanche Sweet's expressions and gestures more clearly and longer than the engineer could have seen them. These emotions carry over into the partial glimpses we have of him, giving added expressiveness and a sense of emotional interrelatedness to all four shots.

If we had seen merely her arm waving out the window, then his arm, and so forth, there would not be enough emotional content. If the engineer had been filmed from inside the train, smiling and waving as she had done, there would be too much emotional content. Sometimes we must try to imagine other ways in which shots or sequences could have been filmed, before we can understand their subtler values. These four shots are put together in a simple, chronological way; they are also dependent upon each other to make sense: because she waves, he waves back; because she throws a kiss, his continued waving signifies a warm, lingering farewell.

An additional element of space is implied in these four shots—the locomotive shot does not merely follow the shot of the girl waving, it is a spatial extension of it. We do not tell ourselves that the train is running across the very place on the screen where the girl was standing in the previous shot (as is more or less true)—we think only of the girl at the window; now, outside the window the train is passing by, and so forth. Like the moving camera in *The Great Train Robbery*, which seems to enlarge our view by panning down the ravine as the robbers escape, editing also extends the size of the screen—not really, but in our imagination.

We do not—and should not—think of all these things when we are watching a film, even for intensive study. But we can try to add one or more of these elements to our conscious observations and our verbal or written recollections, each time we look at it or talk or write about it.

We can hardly miss seeing some of these elements at work in the exciting chase sequence that ends *The Lonedale Operator*. *The Great Train Robbery* also had ended in a chase, filmed in *two long scenes* that lasted about one minute and ten seconds.

The chase at the end of *The Lonedale Operator* lasts some two minutes and forty seconds—and is made up of *37 shots*. Four elements are involved: robbers, girl, engineer, and locomotive.

The possibilities for intercutting are almost limitless; although Griffith establishes a basic pattern, he varies it often enough to avoid monotonous repetition. Increasing the tempo, and occasionally slowing it down, make this exciting action sequence rhythmic and expressive as well.

Space is extended from the girl in the station office to the robbers in the next room, from the engineer inside the moving train to the outside as the train approaches. Griffith asks us to imagine all these transitions in time and place, and we can hardly fail to respond, even today. We are everyone, we are everywhere, and our pulses race all the while. We are no longer looking at moving pictures, we are living them.

Although much of the acting in *The Lonedale Operator* is relaxed and pleasant, some is still stagey and overdone—the robbers and the heroine's father seem particularly tense and exaggerated throughout. Note that we see only as much of each performer as is needed in the shot. Feet magically disappear when they are not needed, but when they help tell the story (as when the heroine is walking on the train tracks), we see them again.

An amusing transformation takes place when the heroine gleefully reveals, in extreme close-up, that the gun she was holding is really a monkey-wrench.

Of the hundreds of other short films Griffith directed for Biograph, only a dozen or so are easily available to the public.

In *The New York Hat* (1912), the camera is now habitually close enough to show subtle changes of expression—longing, surprise, delight. These are a kind of transformation, which appeals both to the eye and to the feelings of the viewer. This was Mary Pickford's last film under Griffith's direction—she had previously appeared in eighty of his movies and was still not yet twenty years old! Lionel Barrymore, already a successful stage actor, has the male lead in this film; it was his first moving-picture role.

In the crowd scenes, many other young stars play bit parts: Mae Marsh, Lillian and Dorothy Gish, Mabel Normand, Mack Sennett, and Robert Harron, all of whom were to be stars themselves, in a very short time. In several of the scenes Mary Pickford shares the close-ups with the ornate hat for which the film is named. "It is a quality, not a defect of the photoplays," wrote Vachel Lindsay in 1915, "that while the actors tend to become types and hieroglyphics and dolls, on the other hand, dolls and hieroglyphics and mechanisms tend to become human."

In 1914, Griffith directed his first four-reel film, *Judith of Bethulia*, soon followed by the even more explosive epics, *The Birth of a Nation* and *Intolerance*. Almost every technique that Griffith adopted was immediately absorbed into general film-making practice. The industry, James Agee wrote, "grew down from him rather than up past him."

In 1919, Griffith joined with Mary Pickford, Douglas Fairbanks, and Charlie Chaplin to form their own distributing company, which they called United Artists; Hollywood businessmen, who by then completely controlled movie-making in the U.S., said that the monkeys had taken over the zoo! Griffith made many successful films in the 1920s, and others that were not successful. His last movie, never released, was made seventeen years before he died; for most of those last years he sat on a park bench in Hollywood, waiting. Perhaps there was nothing more he could discover; meanwhile billions of dollars were being spent to make thousands of movies until all Griffith's discoveries had been milked dry.

He was the first to come close to the face and allow the audience to look into the eyes of the protagonist in thought . . .

. . . and then to flash quickly to the object of the thought.

He was the first to do away with the imaginary proscenium arch, a holdover from the theatre . . .

When criticized for this as he invariably was for every innovation, his answer was that if Dickens could do it in writing, why couldn't he do it also, since they were both painting pictures for the imagination?

—Lillian Gish

pictures for the imagination
pictures for the imagination
pictures for the imagination
pictures for the imagination
pictures for the imagination
pictures for the imagination
pictures for the imagination
pictures for the imagination
pictures for the imagination
pictures for the imagination
pictures for the imagination
pictures for the imagination
pictures for the imagination
pictures for the imagination
pictures for the imagination
pictures for the imagination

The Magic of the Movies

In *The Devil's Wanton* (1948), one of the first films Bergman directed, his heroine watched old movies on a toy projector, while a young man commented on the nature of film—"things suddenly appearing and vanishing, just like our own lives."

The magic of the motion picture is not only that it behaves extraordinarily, but that our reactions are equally extraordinary. We do not read the screen in a literal, logical way—in which case it would make no sense at all—but we are constantly re-adjusting what we see on the screen to make sense and order from it.

When I was ten years old working with my first toy projector, a shaky lantern made of tin—with its chimney, its gas lamp and its continuous films which repeated themselves over and over—I used to find it an exciting and mysterious phenomenon. Even today I feel myself quiver as I did when I was a child, when I consider the fact that actually I am creating illusion. . . . I have at my disposal the most precious and astounding magical device ever put into the hands of a trickster.

—Ingmar Bergman

When a greatly enlarged face appears before us, we do not say, as our great-grandparents said at first, that it is impossible to accept the existence of this huge disembodied head. We believe that it is a normal head that has moved closer to us. We respond to this closeness physically and emotionally, and endow it with new meaning as well.

The editing together of different strips of film also produces magical responses. Just as we do not see the black lines between still images, thanks to our persistence of vision, so we also do not see the abrupt cuts between one succession of images and the next, thanks to what I call our persistence of credulity. In *The Lonedale Operator*, for example, we persist in believing that the girl sees the engineer in the locomotive, that the engineer is waving to her, that these simple actions are interrelated with their own special meanings and emotional values.

As long as we endow these images with connecting links, we do not see the jarring abruptness between shots. It can be seen if you stand so far from the screen that the images are no longer recognizable. I have seen this cutting effect from the distant projection booth of a very large movie theater, and through my window looking at the television set in an apartment across the street. I cannot see it when the images on the screen are recognizable.

It is well known that a group of people witnessing the same accident often give different, or even contradictory, versions of what happened. It is the same with movies; a group of people sitting in front of the same screen does not always "see" the same film. And, of course, our reactions to what we see are always different. We have certain predetermined tendencies to pick out things we like and dislike, according to the type of people we are.

Physical actions stimulate a major response for many people. Hans Richter, a filmmaker and painter who for many years headed the New York City Film Institute, has told a story that well illustrates the physical reaction to movies:

> A German refugee who fled to North Africa in the 1930s managed to take with him a movie projector and one film—a Western. With this he set up a small theater, where many Arabs returned week after week to see the same film. One day he noticed that the reels were out of sequence, that the end of the movie was shown before the beginning, and so on. Yet no one seemed to mind; no one even seemed to notice.
>
> Later he asked one man, whom he knew to be a frequent patron, why no one had complained that the reels were out of order and the story was therefore meaningless. "Oh," replied the man, "we do not come to see a story, we come to see the horses run."

HS·77 (82)

48   From John Ford's *The Horse Soldiers* (Courtesy: United Artists)

Intellectuals have often made fun of Westerns, pointing out the ridiculousness of their plots—or, rather, their plot, since Westerns usually follow a single pattern. But it just may be that there is more beauty in the gracefully moving images of an ordinary grade-B Western than can be found in many more pretentious movies.

Other movies also attract us by their physical aspects—slapstick comedies, gangster and mystery movies, musicals and sports films, films about physical love. We are all physical beings, and to some extent we all respond to physical experiences. But we are also emotional and intellectual beings to some extent. Some of us wish to be moved emotionally rather than through physical actions, and some prefer new ideas to think over.

Whether or not we like a film may depend as much upon ourselves as on the film. But liking or not liking a film is not an important factor in the discovering and learning process. As Canadian Film Board director Tom Daly has pointed out, too often our role as spectator is passive and automatic. We can make it an active, creative role by increasing our ability to see what is on the screen before us.

The more I learn about movies, the more I am also aware of such subtle elements as rhythmic pacing, contrast editing, and intricate form in helping to involve me in the total illusion. Knowing what the film *is about*—that is, its story and action—no longer satisfies me. I also want to know what the film actually *is*.

The films I love most are those I have been able to look at ten, twenty, or thirty times, always finding new elements I had never noticed before. Such films have certain qualities that set them apart from the general run of enjoyable movies. For want of a better word, we usually call these films "great"—but each of us has his own standard for greatness.

One test of greatness in a film is to try to imagine yourself making it, with all the money and time in the world. Such films as Méliès' *A Trip to the Moon* and Griffith's *The Lonedale Operator* belong so inseparably to the men who created them and to the times in which they were made that even a reasonable facsimile seems impossible. Such films, and the many others that are called great, are made not merely with camera and film, but with the life experiences, feelings, and convictions of the men who created them. They seem not to grow old, but magically to grow younger in the course of time.

Charlie Chaplin

Chaplin is a moving picture all by himself before a camera gets in front of him and starts grinding.

—George Jean Nathan

Like Méliès, Chaplin performs magical transformations on the screen, and like Griffith he joins simple actions together to create new meanings and feelings. He does these not with camera tricks or editing techniques, but by using his own fantastic body. Chaplin's short films, particularly those made for the Mutual Company in 1916 and 1917, are all the evidence we need that no performer before or since has possessed so rare a combination of talents: physical agility, emotional expressiveness, and imaginative reflection.

When Chaplin arrived in Hollywood late in 1914, any kind of visual joke was good for a laugh in the movies: a fat lady falling in the street, a dog following a grocery wagon and eating a string of frankfurters, a cop getting hit with a pie. Usually the jokes were repeated over and over again—and they were still funny. But from the start of his movie career, Chaplin wished not only to be funnier than the other comics, he wished to be funny in quite different ways.

"One or two custard pies are amusing enough," Chaplin said later in his career, "but when the picture depends on nothing but custard pies, it soon becomes a weariness. . . . I do prefer a thousand times to get a laugh by an intelligent act than by anything brutal or banal." Not only does Chaplin give meaning to his simple comic movements, but often he endows them with a range of emotions.

In a medium where motion is a basic element, Chaplin soon learned to move his entire body in a distinctive way. Often his movements are so swift that we can hardly see them happening, as in these two moments in *The Cure*, where everyone else is still and Chaplin jumps from one pose to another.

Later in *The Cure*, without props or a change of costume, Chaplin "becomes" a fierce wrestler, then metamorphoses into a dainty bathing beauty.

When Chaplin spills out his cup of mineral water, in the same film, and later pretends that the wet spot was made by a toy dog, he looks at the dog as if he really believes the dog has wet it. And we laugh, because for the moment we can imagine that it is really so.

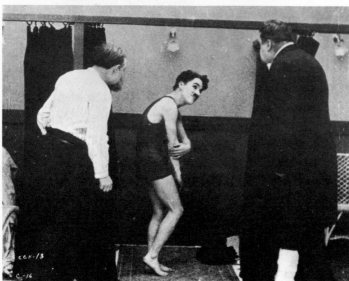

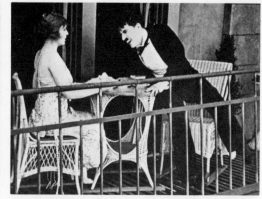

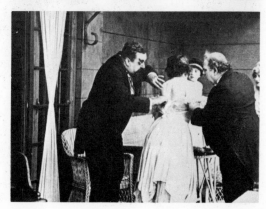

Chaplin also saw the advantages of having one visual joke continue from one shot into another: ". . . when one single happening can by itself arouse two separate bursts of laughter, it's better than two separate happenings doing so," he said. "In *The Adventurer* I succeeded in placing myself on a balcony where I have to eat an ice with a young lady. On the floor beneath I place a stout, respectable, well-dressed lady, sitting at a table. Then, while eating my ice, I let fall a spoonful which slides down my trousers, and then falls from the balcony down the lady's neck. The first laugh is caused by my own embarrassment, the second, and much the greater, comes from the arrival of the ice on the lady's neck."

Sometimes Chaplin could express two thoughts in one continuing gesture—a polite bow in the direction of the beautiful Edna Purviance could turn into a sly kick at Eric Campbell, the bearded villain.

These imaginative transformations of movements and objects reach the virtuoso level in *The Pawnshop*. In a 1917 review of that film, in *The New Republic*, Henry O'Higgins compared Chaplin to a circus clown named Slivers, "who by virtue of a penetrating imagination could see a shoe-lace as anything from an angle-worm to a string of spaghetti, and see it and relate himself to it so convincingly that he made you see it as he did."

"Chaplin performs the same miracle with a walking-stick," O'Higgins continued, "or he is a clerk in a pawnshop, and a man brings in an alarm clock to pledge it. Chaplin has to decide how much it is worth.

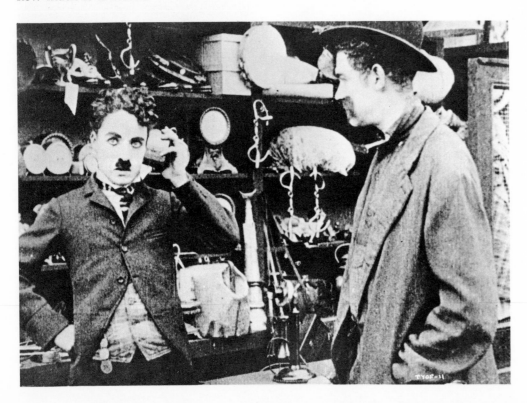

"He sees it first as a patient to be examined diagnostically. He taps it, percusses it, puts his ear to its chest, listens to its heartbeat with a stethoscope, and, while he listens, fixes a thoughtful medical eye on space, looking inscrutably wise and professionally self-confident.

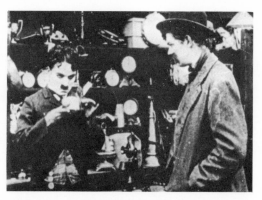

"He begins to operate on it—with a can-opener. And immediately the round tin clock becomes a round tin can whose contents are under suspicion. He cuts around the circular top of the can, bends back the flap of tin with a kitchen thumb, gingerly approaching his nose to it, sniffs with the melancholy expression of an experienced housekeeper who believes the worst of the packing-houses.

"The imagination is accurate. The acting is restrained and naturalistic. The result is a scream."

But the sequence is only half over. Chaplin still dismantles, measures and oils the insides of the clock, which now have begun moving around by themselves, to the great dismay of the would-be borrower, Albert Austin. Finally Chaplin slides the greasy pieces into Austin's hat and returns them to him. When Austin turns to protest, Chaplin hits him on the forehead with a hammer. Even the hammer is not what it seems to be, as Chaplin reveals in a closing moment of the sequence.

This is Chaplin being "a moving picture all by himself," going from one transformation to another with only his gestures and expressions to sustain the illusions. In this sequence that runs nearly five minutes, aside from the close-ups of the can-opener and of Austin's face, there are only three shots!

To fully assess the value of a sequence like this, compare it with a good sequence from any other comedy of your choosing. Funny things happen, to be sure, but rarely on such a sustained level.

It was important that Chaplin arrived in Hollywood just after Griffith had made close-ups and medium shots standard in almost every movie. Had he remained as far from the camera as Méliès usually did, he could not possibly have developed as he did. Although Chaplin did not rely on Griffith's "film language," but preferred to create his own, he referred to Griffith unqualifiedly as a genius.

Although most of Chaplin's subtle gestures are shown in close and medium shots, he found that there is "no set rule that a close-up gives more emphasis than a long shot."

As an example, Chaplin cites this sequence from *The Rink:* "The tramp enters the rink and skates with one foot up, gliding and twirling, tripping and bumping into people and getting into all sorts of mischief, eventually leaving everyone piled up on their backs in the foreground of the camera, while he skates to the rear of the rink, becoming a very small figure in the background, and sits among the spectators innocently reviewing the havoc he has just created. Yet the small figure of the tramp in the distance was funnier than he would have been in a close-up."

Like Méliès, Chaplin played many roles in creating his films. Usually he wrote the story and script, cast and directed the production, played the leading role, and when sound came in composed much of the musical score. But, unlike Méliès, Chaplin has never felt the lack of money in his adult life.

In his fine book entitled *Charlie Chaplin*, Theodore Huff tells us that Chaplin's first movie salary in 1914 was $150 a week, which was three times what he had been earning on the stage. In 1915 he signed a contract with Essanay for $1,000 a week, and in 1916 the Mutual Company offered him $10,000 a week (plus a $150,000 bonus) for his twelve famous two-reelers. Success cannot be measured in money, but it can at least indicate the phenomenal public reaction to this young man, then still in his twenties.

"My whole secret," Chaplin wrote later, "is in keeping my eyes open and my wits wide-awake for everything capable of being used in my films." If it were as easy as that, the movies could have had dozens of Chaplins. It is more likely that Chaplin's success follows the formula given by novelist William Faulkner: "Ninety-nine percent talent . . . 99 percent discipline . . . 99 percent work." The talent can only be marvelled at, but it would be nothing without discipline and work.

Theodore Huff tells us that in making *The Immigrant*, another of his Mutual films, Chaplin shot 90,000 feet of film for a final release that ran 1,800 feet. As the shooting progressed, Chaplin would invite people to come in and look at various sequences—people from the studio or from the street. He knew that he would get laughs, and lots of them. But if the laughs didn't come at the very second he wanted them, he would shoot the scene over and over until they did. No other star or director has put his talents to such demanding tests. Other comedians copied his dress, his mustache, even his name—but none tried to copy what Chaplin actually did in his movies.

Robert Flaherty and *Nanook of the North*

He had perhaps the most gracious eye that ever guided the camera.

—John Grierson

The film of reality, which had its origins in the motion studies of Muybridge and Marey, advanced as far as the newsreel and the travelogue and might have advanced no farther but for the extraordinary discoveries of an explorer named Robert Flaherty.

Reality in the early films had been treated as a phenomenon rather than as an element of creative expression. "A Series of Brilliant and Interesting Scenes absolutely true to life in PRECISION, PROPORTION AND MOTION" is the way the early Lumière programs were advertised. No attempt was made to achieve emotional involvement.

One distinguished reality film was produced as early as 1912. It is a 75-minute film entitled *Ninety Degrees South* (sometimes called *With Scott at the South Pole*), which records the polar expedition led by Captain Robert F. Scott. The photography by Herbert G. Ponting is miraculously sensitive, and the film is a magnificent record of an important event, a handsomely visualized diary of a great scientific expedition that ended in Scott's tragic death. Most of the film's emotional intensity comes from the event itself.

In 1921, Robert Flaherty's *Nanook of the North* showed that the drama of reality could be created especially for film—not with actors and sets, but with real people in their own locations. While Griffith was finishing *Broken Blossoms* and Chaplin was directing *The Kid*, Flaherty was making film discoveries as yet unimagined by anyone.

Flaherty had been a mining engineer and explorer in northern Canada for nearly ten years before he ever held a movie camera in his hands. On his fourth expedition he had taken a camera along, to compile visual notes about the life and habits of the Eskimo people and the country where they lived. He shot some 70,000 feet of film in all (35mm film, to be sure); but some time later the entire negative went up in flame, set off by a lighted cigarette, in an editing room.

Flaherty had edited one print of the material, which he showed to members of the American Geographical Society, hoping that duped copies of the print could be made if the film were successful enough. But it was not. Flaherty himself found it "utterly inept, simply a scene of this and a scene of that, no relation, no thread of a story or continuity whatever." He admitted to himself the most painful discovery of all: "It must have bored the audience to distraction. Certainly it bored me."

Many explorers have subsequently taken cameras along to record their observations and have been entirely pleased with similarly boring results. For Flaherty it was the challenge of his lifetime. "My wife and I thought it over for a long time," he wrote later. "At last we realized why the film was bad, and we began to get a glimmer that perhaps if I went back North, where I had lived for ten years and knew the people intimately, I could make a film that this time would go."

Whatever glimmer may have appeared to Robert Flaherty and his wife Frances, we cannot know. But we can see its results in Flaherty's transition from a declared ineptness to total mastery of a new film medium—the dramatic, imaginative film of reality. From his early trials and errors, Flaherty had learned the importance of seeing his "rushes" while he was filming; material projected on a screen was very different from what one saw from behind the camera. Flaherty spent several weeks at the Eastman Kodak Company, learning to develop and print his film.

Once installed in his hut in Port Harrison, the little trading post that belonged to his sponsor, the French fur company Revillon Frères, Flaherty found that the light from the portable electric plant fluctuated too much for printing the film. So he used daylight instead, letting a frame-sized beam of light through the window and regulating it by adding or taking away pieces of muslin from the aperture of the printer. His Eskimo helpers cut through six feet of ice to get water to wash the film with. It was dried in an annex built next to Flaherty's hut. There was the constant bother of deer hair falling off the Eskimos' clothes onto the film. All these incredible difficulties, which would have defeated any ordinary man, seem only to have strengthened Flaherty's artistic drive and instinct.

It was most important that the film be understood by the Eskimos, who were Flaherty's sole performers and assistants. For many of them, even still pictures were a new experience. They had to be stood in front of a mirror with a photograph held up beside them before they could recognize their own faces. When Flaherty first told them he intended to make a film of them—pictures in which they would move—they roared with laughter. When he told them that more people would see this film than there were pebbles on a beach, they were astonished beyond belief. This laughter and astonishment are vital, elements that almost never recur in a reality film.

With Nanook chosen as chief performer in the film, the walrus hunt was the first sequence to be shot. Three days later Flaherty was able to show it to the Eskimos in the area. At first they were amazed that Nanook could be standing in the picture before them, harpoon in hand, and sitting beside them at the same time. But when the walrus began to move, they became completely involved: "Be sure of your harpoon," they shouted. "Hold him! Hold him!" Then as the walrus was pulled in inch by inch toward the shore, bedlam rocked the house.

Flaherty already had instructed Nanook that in all their work, the film would come first. "Will you remember," he had asked, "That it is the picture of you hunting the iviuk (walrus) that I want, and not their meat?"

"Yes, yes, the aggie (movie) will come first," Nanook had replied earnestly. "Not a man will stir, not a harpoon will be thrown until you give the sign. It is my word."

They shook hands. Never before or since has so great an accord existed between the subject of a movie and its director. The courage, skill, and pride of Nanook in front of the camera seem equally balanced ·by the courage, skill, and pride of Flaherty behind it. So closely related are the spirits of the two men that it seems almost accidental that one man was the director and the other its protagonist.

Nanook of the North is a story of the year-long struggle for survival by an Eskimo family. It might seem that so simple a story could be filmed by anyone who would devote his time and energies to the task and who could endure the physical hardships. But the simplicity of this film is entirely deceptive; such simplicity is so difficult to achieve that no one has succeeded in achieving it in the intervening half-century—indeed few filmmakers have even tried.

What can we find in this seemingly simple portrait of a man and a place that defies imitation and remains forever fresh and exciting? *Nanook of the North* opens with close-up portraits of Nanook and his wife Nyla, followed by an introduction to the sea and land in the summertime and to the baby birds and animals that live there. There is humor and a wonderful sense of movie magic—certainly as enchanting as any transformation by Méliès or Chaplin—in the way Nanook's family appears from inside a seemingly bottomless kayak, one after another.

The sequences continue: trading furs at the post (with a famous scene of Nanook and a phonograph), the walrus hunt, Nanook fishing. Then comes the igloo-building, in which shots of Nanook cutting out the blocks of snow and putting them into place are intercut with shots of Nyla filling in the chinks and shots of their son Allee sliding and playing in the snow. Flaherty's intercutting is as important as Griffith's—not used for speed and excitement, but for involvement and warmth.

Each sequence is a separate incident, yet each builds upon the preceding ones, from summer to winter, from the smiling introduction to the sleeping farewell, until gradually we seem not only to be seeing, but actually to be sharing the lives of those faraway people. Linked together by the same characters and the changing face of the landscape in the rounding of the seasons, these individual episodes become one whole epic poem, which one day surely will rank with the great epics of Ulysses, Beowulf, and Roland. But, unlike these classics, this film poem is easily understood today by anyone, of any age, anywhere —told, as it is, in the language of moving pictures.

In addition to its invincible structure, *Nanook* gains inner strength in many other ways. There are Flaherty's richly varied picture compositions and textures in such shots as the boundless horizon, close-ups of the snarling dogs, Nanook's weathered face, a baby seal. Almost any shot of the film—and of Flaherty's subsequent half-dozen films—could be stopped at any point and enjoyed for sheer pictorial beauty.

Motion in Flaherty's *Nanook of the North* has a magical quality: Nanook running his hand over the sleek blade of his knife; snow transforming the sleeping dogs into soft, white mounds; tiny figures cutting across the snowy vastness. Throughout the film the smallest of Nanook's exploits—catching a fish or releasing a trapped animal—becomes a most delightful adventure, revealed slowly bit by bit until we are almost intoxicated with the excitement of it. When Nanook creeps forward on hands and knees, we are placed in the opposite view, to wait and wonder what new game is being played, what new catch will magically appear.

Photographs from the book *Nanook of the North*, Windmill Books, Inc.

It is not incidental that the only animals we see killed are those Nanook and his family need for food. The cunning white fox is not killed—although against our strongest wishes we can recall that skins such as his were displayed proudly at the trading post. It is an added strength of the film's structure that it takes us farther and farther away from the familiar world of the white man, into the remote world of the primitive man— and from the outer achievements of civilization to the inner workings of the human spirit.

These are only a handful of ways in which *Nanook of the North* is a very special film, and Robert J. Flaherty a very special filmmaker. If you see the film once or twice, or twenty or thirty times, as I have by this time, you will be closer to understanding its uniqueness and its greatness. But you will never completely understand it, any more than you can understand how Nanook can have died in 1923 and still seem to live forever, as this film re-enacts the remarkable story of his life, his time, and his place in the world of men.

From Abstract to Concrete

In the 1920s a number of European artists began experimenting with movies for the first time. Hans Richter described their adventure: "We embarked at that time, like Sinbad the Sailor, on discoveries in the realm of abstract, fantastic, and documentary films." These films were not made for commercial distribution; often they were seen by very small audiences, mainly other artists and filmmakers.

Hans Richter's *Rhythmus 21* and Viking Eggeling's *Symphonie Diagonale* were extensions of the two artists' abstract paintings. Both had already painted on scrolls, on which the eye could create its own rhythmic movements over a wide expanse of changing space, in the fashion of Chinese scrolls. But Richter felt that these scrolls obeyed the laws of painting rather than of motion, and he turned to film, where he could concentrate on "the orchestration of movement and time."

Rhythmus 21 and *Symphonie Diagonale* were made at approximately the same time, and they are the first known abstract films—along with Walter Ruttmann's *Opus I* and *Opus II*. In *Rhythmus 21* we find squares and rectangles, growing larger and smaller, moving across the screen in changing patterns of blacks, whites, and greys, giving us a sense of the basic values of motion alone, without the people and objects we usually see in motion.

Another painter, Marcel Duchamp, who in 1912 had shocked the world with his nearly abstract multiple-image painting entitled "Nude Descending a Staircase," had also begun experimenting with moving designs. In 1925, with the assistance of Man Ray, a still photographer who made some movies of his own, and of Marc Allegret, a French filmmaker, Duchamp made a movie called *Anaemic Cinema*. In it a series of circular designs is set into motion on a phonograph turntable, often giving an extraordinary effect of three dimensions. Between the images Duchamp placed French titles that turn almost too fast to read. One title explains the name of the film: anaemic is an anagram for cinema.

Hans Richter continued with his experimental abstractions for several years, and then began making films about the real world, in which people and objects could move as freely and as fantastically as his lines and shapes had moved.

Ghosts Before Breakfast (9 minutes)
Made by Hans Richter in 1927–28
Ghosts: Darius Milhaud, Paul Hindemith, Jean Oser, Hans Richter, and others.

The film is a delightful combination of Méliès' impossible fantasies and Lumière's everyday realities. Clocks speed ahead, hats fly about in the air, dishes shatter on the ground (and later reassemble themselves), a fire hose rolls itself up, water runs backwards, a line of men walks behind a telephone pole and disappears into thin air, men's faces turn from white to black (by substituting negative for positive film), and dozens of other adventures are enacted in this midway world between fantasy and reality. Then, finally, the men sit down to an outdoor breakfast, hats fly in and rest on their owners' heads, dishes reassemble themselves, and the lackluster world begins as the film ends.

The film was made for a German music festival, with a score by Paul Hindemith that since has disappeared. Richter subsequently wrote about the making of the film:

> Time was short. With a vague idea of using objects as actors—there was no time for a proper script—I started to apply a method I had used before with success: improvisation. I left the responsibility of telling a story to objects. I was prepared to use anything I could discover in the hidden life of these objects.
>
> Four bowler hats—my own and those of my group—were attached to long sticks with fine black twine and waved through the air. They moved with the elegance of pigeons. And they looked alive. The black thread was devoured by the light of the sky. The hats seemed to move by magic or as though they were living their own independent life. . . . Because I believed in them, treated them as living beings, like ourselves, they had "confidence" in me. And since I extended the same faith to all other things as well, they collaborated with me in a sort of fairy tale of the unknown and unseen life of our everyday objects.
>
> And once the theme got going I shot whatever met my eyes: gramophone records, shooting targets, revolvers—and people too. In this fairy tale world there was no such thing as gravity or normality. You had men running up walls, hiding behind no hiding-place, jumping up and down ladders, just everything that could contribute to the dissolution of the bureaucratic harmony and balance in which we spend our daily life.

Ghosts Before Breakfast is a film that stays forever young. "Usually old things go out of style and are forgotten about," a seventh-grade student has written. "But not this movie because it is too good to go out of style."

One of the film's strengths is its balance of sense and nonsense, order and disorder. Each of the joking segments is presented in a rich display of cinematic virtuosity, and miscellaneous segments are linked together, by the use of recurring images, into a well-organized chain of fantastic events. With as much respect as Richter feels toward the objects he has filmed, there is at least equal respect for the mysterious film medium as well.

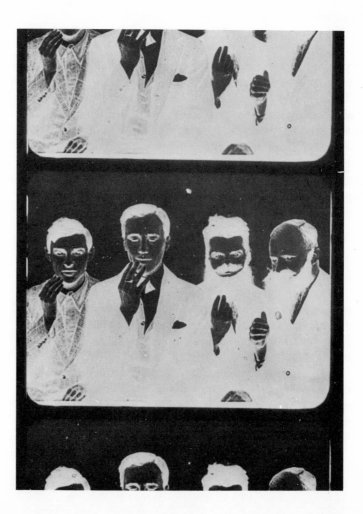

Documentary and experimental films also appeared in the 1920s, with the aim of filming a place or event or substance with as much variation and surprise as the filmmaker could create. Two films of that period use water as their theme:

Rain (15 minutes, silent)
Directed by Joris Ivens and Mannus Franken in 1929

A rainy day in Amsterdam is explored here within a simple chronological framework. The film opens with trees bending in the wind, awnings billowing, and heavy clouds announcing the coming of the storm. As the first drops fall, people scurry along the streets. (Ivens himself appears briefly in this scene.) Ivens got the idea for the film while he was making another film that was constantly interrupted by the rain. Why not use the interruptions to film the rain itself? The subjects proved unusually difficult, since at that time most outdoor filming was done only in full sunlight.

Ivens has written about making the film:

> At that time I lived with and for the rain . . . I organized a system of rain watchers, friends who would telephone me from certain sections of town when the rain effects I wanted appeared. I never moved without my camera—in the office, laboratory, street, train. I lived with my camera and when I slept it was at my bedside table so that if it was raining when I woke I could film the studio window over my bed. Some of the best shots of raindrops along the slanted studio windows were actually taken from my bed when I woke up. . . .

With the swiftly shifting rhythm and light of the rain, sometimes changing within a few seconds, my filming had to be defter and more spontaneous. For example, on the big central square of Amsterdam I saw three little girls under a cape and the skipping movements of their legs had a rhythm of raindrops. There had been a time when I thought that such good things could be shot tomorrow as well as today; but you soon learn that this is never true. I filmed these girls without a second's hesitation. They would probably never again walk at that hour on the square, or when they did it wouldn't be raining, and if it was raining they wouldn't have a cape, or skip in just that way, or it would be too dark—or something. So you film it immediately. . . . It took me about four months to get all the footage I needed for *Rain*. To achieve the effect of the beginning of the shower as you now see it in the film I had to photograph at least ten beginnings and out of those ten beginnings make the one *film* beginning. . . .

In *Rain* I had to remind myself constantly that rain is wet—so you must keep the screen dripping with wetness—make the audience feel damp and not just dampness. When they think they can't get any wetter, *double* the wetness, show the raindrops falling in the water of the canal—make it super-wet.

Rain did teach me a great deal about film emotion . . . I consciously used heavy dark drops dripping in big pear-shaped forms at long intervals across the glass of the studio window to produce the melancholy feeling of a rainy day. The opposite effect of happiness or gaiety in a spring shower could be produced by many bright small round drops pounding against many surfaces in a variety of shots.

I shot the whole film with my old Kinamo and an American De Vry hand camera. My assistant was a young Chinese sailor, Chang Fai, whom I had met as a waiter in a Chinese restaurant on the Zeedyk. . . . I doubt if *Rain* could have been made without Chang's carefully held umbrella and his wonderful black soups that cured the flu—a constant by-product of this film.

The aches and pains that went into the shooting of the film were similarly involved in its editing, with which Mannus Franken assisted at the beginning. The material is real enough, undisturbed except for some shots that seem to have been pre-arranged for the camera. But the editing is, of course, entirely artificial, as Ivens points out, to give the illusion and feeling of a rainstorm, rather than to record a rainstorm.

The opening sequence we might call panoramic, moving as it does from one aspect of the landscape to another—from the ships in the canal to people on bridges to clouds in the sky. Like the shots of the girl and the engineer waving to each other in *The Lonedale Operator*, the arrangement of shots seems to enlarge the screen, horizontally and vertically, until we seem to have taken in the whole expanse of the city as the rain begins.

Another sequence aboard a moving streetcar shows mainly what we would see in front of our eyes—but since we are aboard a moving vehicle, the effect is one of depth. Some sequences are almost purely textural, such as those which show patterns of raindrops on windows, barrels, and elsewhere. These miscellaneous shots grouped into sequences help focus and hold our attention and give meaningful continuity to an otherwise imagistic and poetic rendering of a rainy day in Amsterdam.

Water is the theme of another 1920s film that, as its title indicates, takes a more distant and objective view of the subject.

H_2O (14 minutes, silent)
Made by Ralph Steiner in 1929

H_2O opens with such commonplace shots as falling raindrops, open hydrants, and waterfalls, and then narrows down to the patterns and textures of ocean waves and finally t the surface patterns of nearly still water, light and dark, glitter and drab. Steiner's work in still photography is clearly suggested in the quiet stillness of many shots in the film. Motion is often subtly expressed in still pictures of moving subjects. At its conclusion the film makes the journey back to where we started in Richter's *Rhythmus 21*, from the world of concrete reality to the unrecognizably abstract. *H_2O* is called a film study, and that it is —as well as an illuminating exploration of the abstract form and movement that can be found in every commonplace reality.

From Silence to Sound

We have seen how scientists created the illusion of movement . . . how reality was filmed by the Lumière brothers . . . and dramatized by the explorer Robert Flaherty . . . and poeticized by such experimenters as Joris Ivens and Ralph Steiner. . . . We have witnessed the expansion of the movies' storytelling abilities from Porter's *Great Train Robbery* to Griffith's *Lonedale Operator*. We have entered the fantasy worlds of Méliès, Chaplin, and Richter, and explored their distinctive styles in film.

Throughout these thirty years of movie history, films were generally produced without sound; but in the theaters where they were shown, piano, organ, or orchestral accompaniments were commonplace.

Efforts to record and synchronize sounds with moving pictures had been made since the days of Edison's Kinetoscope. Finally, in 1926, Al Jolson, in *The Jazz Singer*, spoke the memorable line, "You ain't heard nothing yet!"—and almost overnight the movies became the talkies.

Sound-on-film solved some problems: action could flow more smoothly without printed titles; music and sound effects could occur in exact registry; dialogue could eliminate the need for excessively demonstrative acting.

Other problems were added: the camera became static, slave to the unwieldy sound-recording equipment; "talking heads" dominated the screen (as they still do today in television); the movies were once again stage-bound, as they had been in the early pre-Griffith days.

One Russian director made this observation about sound in films: if we see a picture of a dog, we know it is a dog; if we also hear the dog bark, it is no more a dog than it was in the first place. To be truly a creative addition to the moving picture, sound must add new elements, not merely repeat what is shown in the visuals.

Despite a few extraordinarily inventive uses of sound in its early days, talking pictures for many decades found themselves more often than not prisoners of the microphone. Movement, fantasy, even picture quality, were often sacrificed for what was at first the novelty, then later the necessity, of sound.

Some critics thought it was the end of the art of the moving picture. In some ways, it was. But, in the long run, it was not —thanks at least in part to the documentary film movement that began just about the time that sound was introduced.

Documentary films did two important things that studio films often neglected: first, they went out into real locations with real people, giving the camera free range to film whatever it could find, as imaginatively as possible; second, lacking portable sound equipment, they were forced to use sound as creative additions to film rather than as literal accompaniments.

Grierson and the Documentary Movement

Single-handed credit for defining and creating the type of reality film we call the documentary goes to a Scotsman named John Grierson. The word "documentary" was first applied to film in Grierson's review of Flaherty's second film, *Moana,* in 1926. Later he defined it as "the creative treatment of actuality."

Grierson's aim was to use the camera as a window through which the everyday world could be viewed. "We were, I confess, sociologists," he wrote, "a little worried about the way the world was going." Grierson reasoned that if movie theaters did not want to show documentary films, even larger audiences could be found outside the theaters—in schools and colleges, churches, community groups, libraries, and museums—and he helped create a vast non-theatrical film audience throughout the English-speaking world.

Grierson set up two governmental film units in Britain—first at the Empire Marketing Board and later at the General Post Office. These two units gave a large number of enthusiastic and talented men and women the chance to make several hundred short films, dealing directly or indirectly with matters of British trade, communications, and national concern. Although he was the guiding spirit behind most of these films, Grierson himself made only two films. Both are about Scotland's fishing industry. The first is a long silent film called *Drifters,* made in 1929; the second is a short sound film called *Granton Trawler.*

Granton Trawler (11 minutes)
Photographed and produced by John Grierson in 1934
Edited by Edgar Anstey

Theme rather than story holds most documentary films together. Here the theme is man against the sea, in the everyday situation of earning a living. As in *Nanook,* place is an important part of the film—the ship, sea, sky, all are recurring elements. In its treatment of people, however, it is a far cry from *Nanook.* The men in *Granton Trawler* are fishermen and sailors, wage-earners, workers; if they have families, a sense of humor, special temperaments or feelings, we surely don't discover them in this film. Certainly they have no desire to delight or please us. It is *cinéma vérité,* in the sense that little or nothing is done in the film that would not have happened if the camera were not there. (Unlike the cinéma vérité films of today, there was no portable sound equipment at that time; all the sounds we hear in *Granton Trawler*—sea, gulls, whistling—were reproduced in a sound studio—almost a symphony of sounds.)

But the film is not lacking in strengths: the three-dimensional interweaving of the men, the ship, and the elements in the air and sea that surround them; the delicate contrasts of an expansive horizon and the closeness aboard ship; the tenseness of the catch being brought in, and the startling closeup of the fish during the cleaning of the catch.

Like *Rain,* this is an essay in moving pictures. The subject of *Granton Trawler* is somewhat more substantial, dealing with the way men earn their living and the way food is brought in for the survival of us all. It follows a simple chronology: in its opening shots the ship leaves shore; ten minutes later—in screen time—it returns with its catch. Obviously this is not reality, but the illusion of reality, compressing the highlights of many hours into these few minutes by a judicious selection of sights and sounds.

We return with the feeling that we have made a journey aboard a Scottish fishing vessel in the mid-1930s. We have seen it; we have experienced it. To this extent, *Granton Trawler* is a valuable film document, giving a truer and more lasting impression of reality than a realistic newsreel would have given.

When the Empire Marketing Board was dissolved, Grierson was able to move his film unit to the General Post Office with some of his old filmmakers and many new ones. Although most of the productions were largely utilitarian, some were boldly experimental. Here Len Lye made his first dazzling abstract films and Norman McLaren made his first professional movies. In such a film as *Night Mail,* the talents of many artists outside the film world were combined to create new directions for documentary films.

Night Mail (24 minutes)
Produced by John Grierson for the General Post Office in 1936
Directed by Harry Watt and Basil Wright
Sound by Alberto Cavalcanti; music by Benjamin Britten
Verse by W. H. Auden

Before you see *Night Mail*, try to imagine a movie about the overnight mail train from London to Glasgow—or from New York to Chicago, if you prefer. How would it begin, how would it end, and what would happen in the middle to sustain suspense and interest? *Night Mail* begins in a matter-of-fact way, as various behind-the-scenes dispatchers send the train on its way safely and on schedule. We see the train from overhead, from various stations through which it passes, from farms and countryside—while the narrator's voice tells us the facts and figures of the journey.

Only after a change of crew do we get a closer, more personal view of what is happening. The camera moves in to record the men's bantering remarks and gentle shoves, and at last we enter the train where letters are being sorted to be dropped at stations along the way. Some joking dialogue adds a personal touch to this fairly routine part of the work. The tossing of a mail pouch into a catch-all device is dramatized in a brief scene showing a new man being trained for this job. His instructor helps him count the proper number of seconds—and the novice continues the count on his fingers. "Now!" shouts the instructor, and the mail bag is swung outside while the nervous beginner waits to see if his timing was correct.

Many startling sound effects punctuate the film, giving it a vitality that would be lacking if real sounds had been used. As we get nearer the train's destination, Auden's poem reminds us of the routine lives of the people who hear the train pass in the night, of our own involvement in sending and receiving letters, and of our wanting to be remembered.

It has been argued that *Night Mail* is too rich a film, that the meter of the poem conflicts with the meter of the film, that it fails because it tries too hard. Perhaps this is so, but I have yet to see a film that makes an ordinary subject so enjoyable to watch.

John Grierson left the General Post Office Film Unit in 1937 and later went to Canada where he outlined a project that almost miraculously turned into the National Film Board of Canada. As the official film production agency for all departments of the government, it has put Canada on the world's film map, with its outstanding documentaries, animation, experimental, educational, and discussion films, and more recently feature films of social concern. It has lasted over three decades and seems to grow stronger each year. Similar film boards have been started in Australia and New Zealand. (A United States Film Service, which attempted to coordinate American government film production, lasted only a few years.)

The Canadian Film Board alone would be enough to assure John Grierson a place in film history. But his accomplishments are more numerous, and somewhat more difficult to define. By sheer determination Grierson fathered a movement that made the reality film an art form of its own. Not the personal art of a Flaherty, not the trial-and-error art of the avant-garde, but a massive effort to put reality on the screen in the most recognizable and affecting ways that could be found.

Some of the documentary films of the 1930s and 1940s have lost their original importance, but others—like *Housing Problems*, *Song of Ceylon*, and *Listen to Britain* and their American counterparts, *And So They Live*, *The River*, and *Valley Town*—are all the evidence we need of the documentary film's lasting and intrinsic value, and of the movies' indebtedness to John Grierson.

Housing Problems, 1935 (directed and written by Edgar Anstey and Arthur Elton)

Valley Town, 1940 (directed by Willard Van Dyke and photographed by Bob Churchill)

And So They Live, 1940 (directed by John Ferno and Julian Roffman)

Song of Ceylon, 1934–35 (directed, written, and photographed by Basil Wright)

Reality and the Story Film

During World War II, many directors who had worked only with actors in studios were assigned to make documentary films, working alongside documentary directors who had previously dealt only with real people in real places. The result was an inevitable interchange of ideas.

By the late 1940s such powerful films as John Huston's *Treasure of the Sierra Madre* and Roberto Rossellini's *The Open City* had effectively demonstrated that real places and nonprofessional performers (usually in background roles) could add new vitality to the fiction film. It was also possible to see scripted scenes enacted by nonprofessionals in such feature documentaries as *The Quiet One*, by Sidney Meyers, Helen Levitt, and Janice Loeb. Documentary filmmakers were also taking their techniques into the story film, as Harry Watt did in *The Overlanders*, excerpts of which are shown and discussed in a short study film produced by the British Film Institute.

Watt, who had begun making documentary films a dozen years earlier, and who assisted Robert Flaherty in the making of his *Man of Aran*, brought to this feature production many elements of reality that were then new to the fiction film.

The Critic and "The Overlanders" (15 minutes)
Produced by the British Film Institute, with film critic Dilys Powell and excerpts from *The Overlanders*, produced in 1946
Directed and written by Harry Watt

The Overlanders is a story film based on true events in World War II, in which a group of cowmen and a woman drove a thousand cattle across Australia to escape the threat of attack by the enemy. In the scene analyzed here, the cattle have been without water for many days; now they approach a stream whose banks are treacherous quicksand. They must be driven back.

The characters act, dress, and speak in relatively ordinary ways, except perhaps for the stout doctor who supplies welcome comic relief from the mounting tension. Locale plays a large role in filming the story; trees, wind, water are real, and they are shown in a pictorial variety that is somewhat reminiscent of *Rain*. But in *The Overlanders* they are also part of the story.

A first-person narration combines the objectivity of a newsreel with the intimacy of a drama. "It was a stinking hot day," the hero's voice says, as we see him slouching nearly asleep on his horse. "We were dead beat." Such direct feelings could not easily be conveyed in dialogue; nor would it have worked as well if a professional narrator had said: "It was a stinking hot day. The men were dead beat."

The main action, a face-to-face confrontation with the cattle, is shown in a number of shots, which are cut together faster and faster. Critic Dilys Powell, in her analysis, points out how the intercutting of short shots—closer and closer to the camera —gives the sequence an extraordinary tension, which is still evident today. Music heightens the suspense but is intertwined and combined with the lowings of the cattle—again blending drama and reality. "Now!" the hero yells as he flashes his whip in a moment of calm, signalling the men to turn the cattle back from the water. (The same shout occurred at a crucial moment in Watt's documentary, *Night Mail*, you may remember.)

You Can't Run Away (excerpts from *Intruder in the Dust*)
Produced by M.G.M. in 1949
Directed by Clarence Brown; script by Ben Maddow, based on the novel by William Faulkner

Although a number of static "talk" scenes occur in the film, many scenes use film language expertly. The arrival of the sheriff's car early in the film is told in a compelling combination of pictures and sounds. A low-angle shot picks up a moving car as it turns into the town square with men running toward it, and siren sounds further underline its dramatic significance. The repeated thud of a flat tire tells us without words that something is wrong (and at the same time gives us a chance to imagine what it may be, before we are told). Inside the car, from the back seat, we see what the occupants see through the car windows; in the immediate foreground are a pair of black hands in handcuffs. It is almost a symbol of the man's innocence that we are put in his place before we even see him, before we have any clear idea of what is going on.

When the car stops in front of a crowd of people standing by the jail, the sheriff gets out, followed by the prisoner whose hat falls on the ground—and here the picture language ends and dialogue takes over.

But remember that it could have been told in words all along. We could have seen two men watching the car approach, and they could have talked back and forth about the sheriff bringing in a black man who killed a white man, and about the tire that someone had shot to threaten the sheriff and his prisoner. Inside the car we could have seen the prisoner's face as he said the men outside were trying to kill him, and then the sheriff's face saying he would be safe in jail. Visual language is never accidental; it must be planned in the script, in the preshooting arrangements of each shot, and of course in the camera work and the editing.

Later, when lawyer Stevens visits Lucas in jail, dialogue is used with dramatic impact. In the confined space of the cell, the lawyer paces up and down, asking questions and answering them himself, rarely looking his client in the eye. The continuous speechmaking shows that he has no interest in listening to Lucas, in fact that he assumes he is guilty all the while. A bare light bulb hangs from the ceiling, almost as a symbol of reality and truth, which lawyer Stevens ignores.

Even more interesting is the scene where Stevens' young nephew returns to the cell to hear Lucas's story. Their voices speak in dramatic whispers; in extreme close shots we see their eyes, or mouths, or hands clutching at the heavy grille door between them. We need see no more; we already know what they look like. Their enlarged features, spotlighted in distinctive patterns of whites and darks, are visual reinforcement of what they are saying, of the life-and-death relationship between them.

Some of the visuals and sounds seem too contrived, as in the scene of the town square filled with people waiting for a lynching. It is too arranged, too obvious; there is little left to be felt or imagined.

In contrast, the simple inclusion of an old photograph of Lucas as a young bridegroom gives an imaginative dimension to the character of this proud and lonely black man living in a world run by whites.

Intruder in the Dust is probably the best of all efforts to film the novels of William Faulkner, despite its many lapses into static talking scenes. And few portrayals of a black man stand up as well in film as this one, acted by Juan Hernandez, and dramatized throughout by a sensitive script and direction.

Sequences from five Hollywood films of the 1950s are included in a 37-minute compilation entitled *The American Film*. The films were selected by a group of American film critics for the 1966 White House Festival of the Arts. Charlton Heston introduces each segment individually and comments on the director, his objectives, style, theme, and techniques. The words tell us rather little, but we can learn a good deal by looking carefully at the pictures:

The sequence from Fred Zinnemann's award-winning *High Noon* (1952) is essentially silent, music and sound effects having been added later. There is no dialogue, therefore the pictorial variety and editing are not measured to the length of a sentence. Tension mounts as the good guys and bad guys wait for the noon train, which is bringing in a killer who has sworn to "get" the sheriff, played by Gary Cooper. A variety of close-ups of faces, long shots of empty streets and railroad tracks, some quite exaggerated angles of the killer's henchmen are intercut faster and faster to create a physically and emotionally involving scene. It is noteworthy that Zinnemann had begun his movie career in documentary films, and his cameraman, Floyd Crosby, had an extensive and outstanding background in documentaries (including parts of Pare Lorentz's *The River* and Flaherty's *The Land*, both of which were made for departments of the United States Government).

Tension in Alfred Hitchcock's *North by Northwest* (1959, color) is of a completely different kind. While *High Noon* is constructed of a number of short bits of realistic elements (somewhat on the pattern of *The Lonedale Operator*), this scene attains its effect mainly through contrivances that are fantastically bold (something like *Rescued from an Eagle's Nest*). Editing can only go back and forth in a chase scene that is restricted to two elements—the hero, Cary Grant, and the airplane, with its invisible villains. When the plane approaches, we see it; when the hero runs or hides, we see him. The effect is terrifying, but mainly physical. There is little for us to imagine. Never mind, the director seems to be thinking, I'll do the imagining for you. All we have to do is sit there, and be terrified nearly to death—as people were when they saw Lumière's train coming into the station!

William Wyler's *Friendly Persuasion* (1956, color) illustrates well the unfortunate results of using artificial scenery and settings in a warm, personal drama. The photography is inevitably a series of static "talk" shots, relying on words rather than pictures or motion to tell its story. There is nothing to photograph except the actors' faces. The film's appeal rests largely on the personalities of the actors and on the story as it unfolds in dialogue.

The sequence selected from Elia Kazan's *On the Waterfront* (1954) shows Rod Steiger and Marlon Brando as brother hoodlums, inside a simulated limousine, talking, talking, talking. The audience sits and listens, nothing to look at except the faces of the two men, rarely changing expression, and the occasional flashes of light supposedly representing cars and street-lamps passing by. Despite its attempt at natural dialogue, for which Kazan is said to have had the actors improvise their lines, the isolated effect of such a sequence is drawn-out and lifeless.

The shots of Charlton Heston, as on-camera narrator, are similarly static and unimaginative. If Heston's movie career had consisted of shots like these, he could not have become a famous star. The fact seems to be that movies must move, one way or another, fast or slow, dramatically or realistically; the director who forgets this makes his audiences suffer the consequences.

The closing scene from George Stevens' *Shane* (1953, color) ends this compilation of sequences. It is a gunfight action scene, witnessed by a small boy who then watches his hero, Alan Ladd, ride off toward the horizon, and calls out after him, "Shane . . . Shane . . . Come back, Shane. . . ." In this touching moment, Mr. Stevens, who was a cameraman before he began directing movies, creates a memorable visual blending of motion and emotion, without placing an excessive burden upon his actors.

The short story film, which lends itself well to experimentation, is a rarity in film history, mainly because such films rarely repay their production costs. *An Occurrence at Owl Creek Bridge* is an outstanding exception, since it earned large sums of money in movie theaters, on television, and in 16mm distribution—as well as numerous awards, including a Hollywood Oscar.

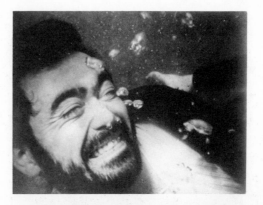

An Occurrence at Owl Creek Bridge (27 minutes)
Produced by Marcel Ichac and Paul de Roubaix in 1962
Directed by Robert Enrico

Based on a short story by Ambrose Bierce, this is an unusually sensitive adaptation, in film language, of the last moments in the life of a young Southerner during the American Civil War. It is an outstanding film, but one not without weaknesses. Several scenes are too long and are overplayed: when, for example, an off-screen voice sings, "I Want to be a Living Man," or when the hero laughs too wildly and clutches too desperately at the ground, or when he runs through woods and fields.

But there is much to be said in the film's favor. Basically it is a film of contrasts: of loud and soft sounds and music, of extreme long shots and close-ups, of startling pictorial contrasts in blacks and whites, of running movements and stillness, of striking movements away from the camera (the hero going over the rapids) and toward the camera (the hero running down a road lined with tall trees), of realistic details (the soldiers' duties at the hanging) and fantasy-dreams (the hero's wife shown in slow motion, and his final effort to reach her, repeated three times). The interplay of these contrasting elements makes it possible for us to believe, throughout the film, something we know is not possible—that a man can survive his own hanging.

The Bierce story opens in this way:

> A man stood upon a railroad bridge in northern Alabama, looking down into the swift water twenty feet below. The man's hands were behind his back, the wrists bound with a cord. A rope loosely encircled his neck.

A literal scenario would have followed the story in the same way: man on bridge; water below; hands tied behind back; rope around his neck; and so on. All these shots do occur in the film, but they have been placed where they will have fullest dramatic impact in cinematic terms.

The movie opens with a shot that explains the basic plot of the film; but the style is so factual that in the course of the story's unfolding we are able to forget it completely. It is the shot of a poster announcing that any civilian caught interfering with the railroad will be summarily hanged. In the next shot the camera moves through wintry woods to a burned-out bridge, and on to another bridge, as unseen owls hoot in the early dawn. Nearer and nearer we go, asking ourselves what possibly can be happening, until we are brought to witness an execution in painfully minute detail. Witness, but not believe, because without our knowing it the film has already created an atmosphere in which reality and fantasy are invisibly intertwined. This is what gives the film its unusual strength, together with the sensitivity of the leading actor (Roger Jacquet) in most of his scenes, the fine eye of the director and cameraman in placing figures in the landscape, and the occasionally brilliant timing of shots and sequences in what is basically a race against death.

It is interesting to compare this film with two earlier versions of the same story: *The Bridge*, an 11-minute film produced by Charles Vidor in 1932, and a 17-minute color production entitled *An Occurrence at Owl Creek Bridge*, produced by graduate students at the University of Southern California in 1956.

Of *The Bridge*, Lewis Jacobs has written:

> The picture opens with the spy (Nicholas Bela) walking between the ranks of a firing squad. Everything seems quite casual, except for a slight tenseness in the face of the spy. A bayonet is driven into the masonry, the rope is fastened, the command is given, the drums begin to roll, the commanding officer orders the drummer boy to turn his face away from the scene, the noose is placed, the victim climbs to the bridge parapet. Now the drumbeats are intercut with the spy's beating chest. Suddenly there is a shot of a mother and child. At this point the unexpected occurs. The noose seems to break and the condemned man falls into the river. . . .

The Bridge was shot in natural locations, Jacobs tells us—but a comparison with the French version shows how little they were used to create a counterpoint between the realism and the fantasy of the story. The straightforward cutting style of *The Bridge* produces an entirely different effect from the strikingly effective contrast cutting in Enrico's film.

The U.S.C. student production of *An Occurrence at Owl Creek Bridge* is surprisingly well made, within its own terms, but it lacks the subtly contrasting elements that make the French version outstanding. Its color adds very little to the overall effectiveness of the visual elements—in fact, it is considerably less expressive than the black-and-white, in both the realistic and the fantastic aspects of the story. It would be profitable to look at this film for its color values alone, seeking out those shots and sequences that are enriched by color and those that seem overcharged.

"The most interesting films," poet John Gould Fletcher has written, "are those in which reality and fantasy are in some way interwoven in the very stuff of the story."

The Art of Animation

As the invention of perspective had revolutionized painting in opening to the painters of the Renaissance a way into a new dimension—that of depth—the invention of animation offers to the painters of our day the new dimension of movement.

—Alexander Alexeieff

A one-reel film, lasting approximately ten minutes, is composed of some 14,000 individual images. In a live-photoplay film, these images are recorded mechanically, 24 times a second, and are taken from real-life substances and actions. In an animated film, the images are usually created individually—substance, movement, and all. The task is herculean, calling for incredible patience and dedication, and an extreme sensitivity to motion itself. As one animator has said, it is not to motion alone that the animation artist must give his attention, but to the individual phases that make up each motion.

In this chapter we call attention to the films of four outstanding animators whose techniques and achievements are unique in movie history: Oskar Fischinger, Len Lye, Carmen D'Avino, and Alexander Alexeieff.

Oskar Fischinger's "absolute film studies" originated in his efforts, at the age of nineteen, to analyze and graph the flow of feelings and events in Shakespeare's *As You Like It* for the members of a literary club to which he belonged. The experiment was fascinating, he later reported, but most people found it unintelligible. Fischinger felt that what was needed to make it understandable was motion.

After several years' experimentation with films using wax, liquids, and paintings on glass, Fischinger created his series of Film Studies. These were abstract films made of individual charcoal drawings on white paper—some 1,500 per minute of film—photographed one by one and printed in negative, so that what we see are white figures against a black background.

As Richter and Eggeling had done a few years earlier, Fischinger set simple forms into motion, with one important change: the visual elements were composed and animated in exact synchronization with their accompanying musical backgrounds.

Norman McLaren recalled that he was also dreaming of forms that would move to musical rhythms when he was still in art school, making his first experiments with moving pictures. Then he saw one of Fischinger's early Film Studies:

> This particular film I saw was to Brahms' *Hungarian Dance No. 6*, I think, and it was entirely abstract, but very fluid abstraction . . . and this was for me like the realization of a dream. I dreamt of forms, and here was someone else dreaming of different forms to music, but he actually had turned it into a movie. I was greatly influenced by that film.

In *Film Study #6* (2 minutes, 1929), set to a jazz recording of the period, we enter an abstract, three-dimensional world created entirely by the artist's ingenuity and imagination. There is delightful interplay of half-moon shapes swinging and swaying in rhythmic motions; of rectangles that seem to turn in mid-air, like sheets of paper, then dissolve into a vanishing line; of circles that shrink into dots, which then burst explosively.

In *Film Study #7* (3 minutes, 1929), set to Brahms' familiar *Hungarian Rhapsody*, similar shapes appear, along with new ones that also dance in a seemingly three-dimensional space. The movement is controlled, yet free—calculated, yet light-hearted.

Film Study #8 (5 minutes, 1930), set to Dukas' *Sorcerer's Apprentice*, is a longer, more involved composition with some lovely configurations of straight and curved lines, again using the entire screen space as a three-dimensional setting for this visual dance.

In the early 1930s Fischinger began his color abstractions, but, as he later wrote, "I soon found out that the simplicity of my own black-and-white films could never be surpassed."

Fischinger came to the United States from Germany in 1936 and settled in Hollywood, movie capital of the world. His almost futile efforts to find work in these later years are but another sorry example of the struggle between creative film artists and businessmen-employers.

In all of Fischinger's films there is delicacy and variety in movement and design. Generally those that are shortest, with the fewest visual elements, are the most enjoyable to watch. But all are worth seeing as examples of a great talent at work, and as exercises in understanding the value of pure motion in moving pictures.

"One of the few original filmmakers," Lewis Jacobs has written, "Fischinger represents the first rank of cinematic expression in the nonobjective school."

"Who is Len Lye?" a young "underground" filmmaker is said to have asked, unaware that he was inquiring about the world's foremost pioneer in cameraless animation, and one of the liveliest, farthest-out, and most inventive animators of all times. As a boy in New Zealand, Len Lye experimented with motion by making sketches while sitting in a slow-moving horse-drawn cart, and by building mobile constructions with pulley wheels turned by an old phonograph handle. At twenty-one he learned cartoon animation in an Australian studio, then he spent two years in Samoa captivated by primitive life and art. He subsequently turned up in London, "a rolling stone in art, journalism, poetry, and philosophy," as Edgar Anstey described him. (And a rolling stone in the 1920s was a rolling stone indeed!)

The London Film Society put up money for Len Lye's first film, *Tuslava*—which means in Samoan "things go full cycle." Later, begging discarded clear film from friends at Ealing Studios, he persuaded John Grierson and Alberto Cavalcanti at the G.P.O. Film Unit to let him make abstract moving designs directly on the film, synchronized to rhythmical popular music. To conform with the public-service nature of Grierson's unit, the films included written messages such as "Post Before 2 P.M." or, in wartime, "The Enemy is Listening to You," always inventively integrated into the rest of the film.

In *A Colour Box* (5 minutes, color), made in 1935, Len Lye stencilled patterns of dots and lines across strips of film, to the rhythms of a contemporary jazz score. The total effect is spontaneous and wild. Norman McLaren has called it "the prime ancestor of all cameraless films" and the "spiritual and technical grandfather" of his own abstract films. McLaren also has pointed out that Len Lye not only discovered a highly original way of adding color to his basically black-and-white images, but he also made really exciting and creative use of it. (It is interesting that McLaren uses this same system to add color to his own films, many of which were shot in black and white.)

Color is a brilliant element in Len Lye's *Trade Tattoo* (6 minutes, color), made in 1937, with a variety of visual effects that no one since has attempted to handle. The film combines live-action photography of workers and machines with stunning color designs painted or stencilled over them with a splendor and irrationality that would certainly have thrilled the great magician Méliès. The shots of the workaday world were salvaged from out-takes of various documentaries that other G.P.O. film people had made; their footage has never been more dramatically immortalized. (See color picture on page 105.)

"I believe a great film, like a great work of art, can be made out of any subject matter whatever," Len Lye wrote. "It is the style and the state of mind of the creator reflected in his work that matters; not the clay pipes, mountains, sea waves, sunflowers, or the birds of his subject." Flaherty's *Nanook* and Grierson's *Drifters* were of lasting consequence, Len Lye points out, because the filmmakers showed subconscious preoccupation with the significance of life, rather than with fur or herring.

Since coming to the United States in the early 1940s, Len Lye has had pitiably few opportunities to make films that are significant to him. *Free Radicals*, which he financed himself in 1958, won first prize ($5,000) at the Brussels Experimental Film Exposition. It was etched by hand, with a needle, frame by frame, its white figures jiggling rhythmically against a black background to a soundtrack of African ritual drumming and chants. The film has been shown infrequently in this country because Lye feels that artists are not paid fair prices for their films. "A museum will pay several thousand dollars for a piece of sculpture," he explains, "but it asks the artist to loan or give his films for nothing." In recent years Len Lye has turned to experimental motorized sculptures, a field in which he has gained considerable recognition.

Still, with his own money, time, and resources, he does continue working on a film tentatively titled *Particles in Space*, which he describes as an extension of *Free Radicals*. "A free radical," Lye has said, "is a fundamental particle of matter which contains the energy of all chemical change, very much like a compressed spring before release." I can't think of a better answer, if one is needed, to the question, "Who is Len Lye?"

Len Lye's films must be seen to be believed: an exquisite and subtle range of vibrating color; an enchanting and original synchronization of visual images and gay music; a brilliant interweaving of live-action shots, special photographic effects such as photo-montage, solarization, and silhouette, and lettering, drawing, stencilling, stippling, painting, all done in direct technique (i.e., directly onto film, without being photographed). His films are made with a perfect sense of rhythm, pace, and composition, and best of all they possess a quality often lacking in the experimental film—wit.
—Adrienne Mancia and Willard Van Dyke
in *Art in America*

Winning a $100 grant from the Creative Film Foundation was "a great boost to my morale," D'Avino has stated. More and more he turned from painting to filmmaking. Today he makes a living from commercial assignments and uses his spare time and money to make personal films. *The Room, Stone Sonatu,* and *Pianissimo,* among others, established a D'Avino style that, according to Jonas Mekas, makes you want to jump up and down, to sing, to run out into the streets with a bucket of paint and brushes, and paint all over the walls. (See color strip on page 105.)

The Room (about 6 minutes, color) is unmistakably D'Avino, a color fantasy in which invisible hands metamorphose a drab New York City room into an ecstasy of color. Walls, radiators, even the ceiling, become magically transformed. The joyous feeling is all the more amazing when we realize that like all animators D'Avino must work very slowly. It took two whole days to color the radiator alone. D'Avino painted about one half-inch strip at a time, then stopped to shoot one or two frames in the camera (usually tripping over the tripod in between, he adds). Climbing the ladder to paint the ceiling, and then climbing down to shoot pictures was a "horrible experience" that took much longer to complete. (Unfortunately there is no film of D'Avino working on *The Room*; it sounds at least as zany as *The Room* itself!)

Carmen D'Avino was a painter in post-World War II Paris, where he took a film course at the Ecole de Cinématographie and shot an unfinished film about a group of fellow American artists. When he returned to the U.S., he got a job in a factory and in his free time made his first animation film. He choose animation rather than live shooting because he could experiment at home with all kinds of materials—drawings, matchsticks, sequins, clay, and others. Then, and now, he created all his optical effects in the camera, including dissolves and double exposures.

In *Tarantella* (3 minutes, color), one of his most recent films, D'Avino used cutouts of photographs and drawings from magazine and newspaper ads, intercut with animated drawings and some real shoes and feet, to capture the rhythms of this lively Italian dance. In all his films, D'Avino works entirely alone. He designs, plots, animates, and photographs his own films, enjoying the freedom that this approach gives him. D'Avino says he makes these films for the fun of it, and he hopes that audiences derive as much fun from them as he does.

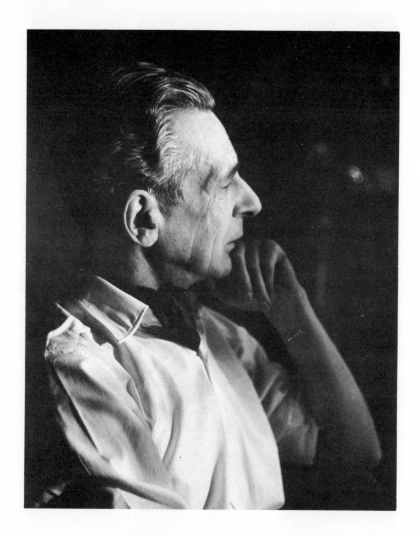

The Russian-born French artist Alexander Alexeieff tells us that he began to draw at the age of four, making scenes of boats crossing the Bosphorus—where he spent his childhood— of warriors running to attack forts, and of galloping horses in profile. Later, he drew series of pictures in a little notebook, phase by phase: a windmill with turning arms, an airplane taking off and landing. These he calls his first films. In Paris in the 1920s Alexeieff began his artistic career first as a set designer for theater and ballet, then as an engraver of illustrations for books by such writers as Gogol, Dostoyevsky, Tolstoy, Poe, Malraux, and more recently Boris Pasternak. It was after seeing some of the avant-garde films of the period—most notably Bartosch's *L'Idée* and Léger's *Ballet Mécanique*—that he turned seriously to filmmaking; that is, to the animated film.

Using a technique of his own invention, which he calls the Pinboard, Alexeieff created his first film, *Night on Bald Mountain*, based on Moussorgsky's tone poem. The film was made in 1933 and lasts eight minutes. Although the original negatives have long been lost, the prints that exist today still reveal astonishing effects in three dimensions; in gradations of blacks, whites, and greys; and in fantastic transformations.

Norman McLaren has singled out this film as "first and foremost" on his list of the world's best animated films—for its uniqueness, for its great poetic quality, for its magical metamorphic imagery and surrealist fantasy, for its unusual technique of using fully animated chiaroscuro, and for its capturing of the spirit and nuances of Moussorgsky's music. "Above all," McLaren concludes, "it is the quality of Alexeieff's imagination that stirs me profoundly."

Night on Bald Mountain is an extremely complex film, one that must be seen at least half a dozen times before it can really be seen at all.

Alexeieff has made two other films on the Pinboard, a very short one produced by the National Film Board of Canada (*En Passant*, no longer in distribution) and *The Nose*, a recent creation. He is at present working on a trilogy of three short films based on Moussorgsky's *Pictures at an Exhibition*. For study purposes, *The Nose* is the best introduction to Alexeieff's style and technique.

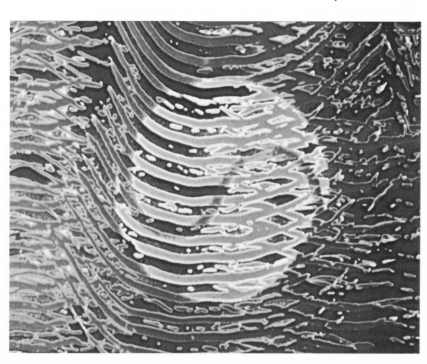

Left:
16mm strip from Carmen D'Avino's *Pianissimo*

Right and center:
Strips from Alexander Alexeieff's two-minute commercial, *La Sève de la Terre*

Len Lye's *Trade Tattoo*

The Nose (11 minutes)
Created by Alexander Alexeieff, assisted by Claire Parker, in 1963
Produced by Cinéma Nouveau, Paris; music improvised by Hi-Minh

Nikolai Gogol's short story tells of a barber who finds a nose in a loaf of bread, a young man who awakens noseless, and the nose itself, which attempts to take on a gentlemanly life of its own. "Such things do happen," Gogol wrote at the end of the story, "not very often, but they do happen."

In adapting literature to film, Alexeieff does not attempt to re-tell the story, but to give it a new life in a new medium. On first viewing we may look for those elements that help create the continuity—this happened, then that happened, and so forth. But in subsequent viewings we can see how Alexeieff creates a fantasy world uniquely his own, one that is quite independent of the story outline. In Alexeieff's fantasy world, almost everything behaves unnaturally:

> Time, for example, is speeded up when the sun races across the morning sky; time slows down when the hero attempts to coax the nose back onto his face.

> Objects transform themselves into other objects, or into people, when a couch becomes a rowboat in the hero's dream, or a streetlamp becomes a policeman in the barber's imagination.

Stationary objects can move or disappear at will, as when walls open to the street, revealing passersby who peer in at the noseless man.

A mysterious black figure rises from below the street, personifying some unknown presence that observes what goes on, without our knowledge.

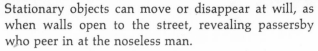

The nose itself undergoes many transformations: first it lies lifeless in the bread; later it attaches itself to the side of the guardhouse; next it grows larger, underwater, face to face with a fish; then it appears man-sized, dressed elegantly with a life and a will of its own.

In these respects, and nearly all others, *The Nose* is a fantasy created in film, not the re-telling of a well-told story. "I hate the very term of story," Alexeieff has said. To transpose the twenty pages of Gogol's story into eleven minutes of screen time, Alexeieff reduced its seven characters to three main ones, compressed fourteen days into twenty-four hours, and dropped three-fourths of the text. The film was made as a silent film, almost as a pantomime; music was added later, for punctuation rather than for melody or rhythm.

The Pinboard on which Alexeieff creates his extraordinary black-and-white films is an upright perforated board, three by four feet, into which a million headless steel pins have been inserted. When the pins are pushed forward and lighted obliquely, they create an entirely black surface on the front of the Pinboard. When they are pushed back, the white of the board shows through. In between, the pins create various shades of grey.

In the film entitled *Alexeieff at the Pinboard* (8 minutes), you can watch the artist and his wife during the designing of still illustrations for the book, *Doctor Zhivago*. Using engravers' tools and simple homemade implements like curtain rings and tops of cold-cream jars, they make simple pictures of an apple or a fir tree. Alexeieff also shows how he transforms day into night, and adds snow to a landscape—calling out instructions to Claire Parker who controls the back of the board, from where she sees the negative reversal of the blacks and whites.

To make a film, many thousands of individual pictures must be created and photographed frame by frame; the artists can see only the last picture, which remains on the Pinboard. The equivalent in writing would be to write a novel with all sentences except the last locked into a box from which they could not be withdrawn until the completion of a chapter. It seems impossible, but Alexeieff has proved that he can create films this way. It is not by accident that Alexeieff has been called "the Einstein of animation."

A newly added sound track (the film was originally released without commentary) gives the artists' own explanations of their work and technical procedures, as well as some of their creative thoughts about animation.

In addition to his independent films and his many book illustrations, Alexeieff has made many brief commercials, in color, always using some unusual animation technique. "I console myself that there really is an 'art' of selling," Alexeieff has said. "It pleases me to construct over a period of four months a synthesis whose presence on the screen will last only one minute during which the audience cannot withdraw its attention for a fraction of a second."

Alexeieff has made several dozen of these short films for showing in European movie theaters (not for television). Their musical scores were written by such composers as Milhaud, Auric, and Poulenc, and they are classed among the finest of "miniatures" in film.

Among his most esteemed commercials is *La Sève de la Terre* (1955), a super-commercial that runs nearly three minutes and involves many kinds of animation. In it letters revolve and disappear in a sandy desert, a derrick-tree produces fruitlike oil droplets (made of hand-blown glass, phase by phase), and Alexeieff displays a special technique of illusory solids, which he himself invented. (See color strips on page 105.)

Norman McLaren and the Essence of Animation

What is the essence of animation? It is what happens between each frame of film—this is what is all-important.

—Norman McLaren

Norman McLaren has explored more kinds of movements, more themes, and more moods of animation in films than anyone else in movie history. He has painted, scratched, stencilled, and drawn on clear film and on black film, with and without regard to frame lines; he has animated cut-out papers, real objects, even people; he has filmed frame-by-frame changes of a single pastel drawing, made people look like the abstract diagrams of Dr. Marey's early moving-picture experiments, and created his own handmade sound tracks by drawing along the side of the film; he has experimented with the principles of persistence of vision, designed repeated movements through multiple-printing—and in all these varied techniques, and innumerable combinations thereof, he seems comfortably and effortlessly creative.

McLaren is the first to acknowledge that he probably is not the first person to do any of these things, and he mentions among his spiritual and technical creditors Méliès, Emile Cohl, Fischinger, Len Lye, Alexeieff, and many others—including John Grierson ("for he gave me a chance to work, encouragement, and freedom"). He also acknowledges the valued collaboration of many other Canadian Film Board artists with whom he has worked. "Sometimes I get the impression from articles people write about me that I make my films almost singlehanded," he has said. "Now, this is a quite erroneous impression. Usually it's with one or two people. We form a small team. Most often it's been Evelyn Lambert, but almost as frequently with Grant Munro. On the music side it's with Maurice Blackburn."

Technical virtuosity is only one part of McLaren's artistic strength; he also ranges in mood from the most delightfully carefree to the most gravely alarming. His films are enriched with an abundance of childish playfulness, artistic subtlety, psychological insight, and human concern.

But all these talents do not make a great animator. The uniqueness of McLaren comes from an unrivalled capacity for making everything move, with meaning and with feeling. "Under his fingers," Tom Daly has said, "a chair becomes tender, hopeful; or the figure 2 is insulted, frustrated, triumphant." McLaren's chairs and numbers, lines and people, take us back to the days of Méliès, when film was a free medium in which anything could happen.

Norman McLaren began making films at art school in Scotland, when he was still in his teens, using second-hand film and a borrowed camera. These independent efforts won him a place in Grierson's General Post Office Film Unit in London, where he directed live-photography films and made several animated ones—about the telephone directory, airmail postal services, and the like. In New York at the beginning of World War II, he worked briefly with filmmaker Mary Ellen Bute and made his own abstract color films under grants from the Guggenheim Museum of Non-Objective Art (which also supported Oskar Fischinger in some of his undertakings). These films were released later under the titles *Stars and Stripes*, *Boogie Doodle*, and *Loops*.

In 1941, John Grierson invited McLaren to join the newly formed National Film Board of Canada, where he has remained ever since, setting up a large and productive animation department, and inspiring and helping to train a generation of younger animators.

"Perhaps it was because I was born and brought up in Scotland that I have always been interested in small budget films. I certainly admit that I get a distinct pleasure from making a film out of as little as possible in the way of money, equipment, and time."

McLaren's earliest films are not circulated in the U.S.—but their titles (*Camera Makes Whoopee*, *Love on the Wing*, *Dollar Dance*, for example) are refreshingly amusing to contemplate. McLaren's first worldwide success came with the delightfully abstract *Fiddle-de-dee*.

Fiddle-de-dee (4 minutes, color)
Made by Norman McLaren, at the National Film Board of Canada, in 1947

A country fiddle playing "Listen to the Mockingbird" sets the tune and mood for this lively assortment of moving color patterns, made entirely without a camera. Most of the images are frameless—i.e., painted on long strips of film, without regard to the intervening frame-lines. Some strips were textured by scratching, stippling, or pressing with cloth before the paint had dried. Double effects were sometimes achieved by painting both sides of the film in different colors, with images seeming to flow simultaneously in opposite directions—a giddy sensation, to say the very least.

Even the one-way movements go in all directions—up, down, sideways—using the element of motion to the fullest possible extent. Sometimes little designs of spirals, lines, or chicken-feet are painted or scratched onto the individual frames, enriching the picture content with amusing surprises. According to McLaren, *Fiddle-de-dee* is a film that speaks only to the senses.

Le Merle (5 minutes, color)
Made by Norman McLaren, in collaboration with Evelyn Lambert
Music arranged by Maurice Blackburn
Produced by the National Film Board of Canada in 1958

McLaren's cut-out crow is one of the most delightful and unforgettable birds in movie history, made up of circles, lines, and angles constantly on the move, dancing around the screen, reshaping themselves into ever new forms and images.

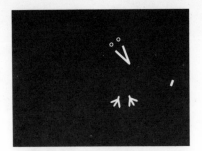

Set to the music of a French-Canadian folksong, admirably sung by the Trio Lyrique of Montreal, it tells of a nonsensical crow who, in each verse, loses a part of his body—beak, head, and so on—only to have it reappear three times. In each verse the parts of the crow accumulate, and by the end of the film the bare outline of a crow has turned into a wild conglomeration.

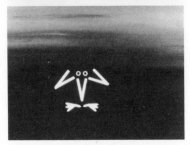

Such a plan, if followed methodically, could end up as tiresome repetition, nonsense or no nonsense. But McLaren uses all his imaginative powers to provide continuous and unexpected movement, amusing transformations, changing backgrounds, and an increasingly faster pace.

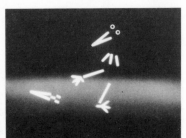

The transformations are easy enough to point out: an eye becomes a bouncing ball, or the crow itself changes into a game of tic-tac-toe. But less evident are the background changes in color and texture; in one sequence a remarkable three-dimensional effect seems to take us into outer space.

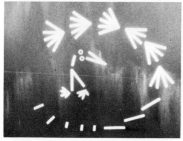

Every inch of the screen is set into motion as the crow leaps and slides this way and that across the landscape, while the camera seems to rise up and later fall back to earth.

From a weird, impossible-looking creature, the body parts spin out into increasingly abstract patterns, before finally falling and scattering in all directions.

All these diversions, many of which we hardly notice when we watch the film, set it apart from ordinary animated films into a unique category all its own. It is not design that makes *Le Merle* outstanding, or even color (which was added later), but movement itself—which creates a vitality and a weightlessness that carry us almost to the limits of our wildest dreams. And to think that each element of each movement was moved individually, by hand, and filmed one frame at a time! It hardly seems possible. (See color strip on page 116.)

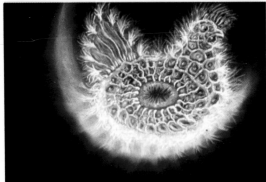

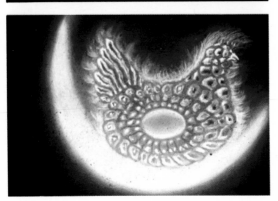

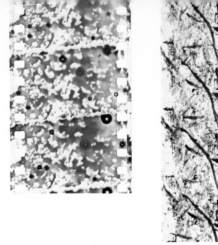

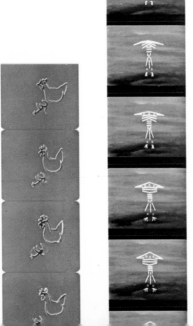

Above:
35mm strips from Norman McLaren's
Begone Dull Care

McLaren's chickens, hens, and birds
from left to right: *La Poulette Grise,*
Hen Hop, and *Le Merle*

Begone Dull Care (7 minutes, color)
Made by Norman McLaren in 1949

Using many of the techniques of *Fiddle-de-dee*, this film is considerably more sophisticated visually and musically. Subtitled
"A Caprice in Color," it combines frameless moving lines with
various textured patterns, synchronized rather loosely to the
"cool" jazz of the Oscar Peterson Trio. Occasional figures
scattered here and there point the way to the subliminal experiments yet to come in *Blinkity Blank*. As in McLaren's other
hand-painted films, no camera work was involved in the production of *Begone Dull Care*. Prints were copied directly from
the original 35mm strips on which McLaren and his associate,
Evelyn Lambert, worked.

A Chairy Tale (10 minutes)
Made by Norman McLaren; sitar music by Ravi Shankar
Co-directed with Claude Jutra
Produced by the National Film Board of Canada in 1957

A young man (Claude Jutra) tries to sit down on a kitchen chair to read his newspaper, but he soon learns that the chair has other ideas. Using all the known human ways of coaxing, cajoling, and forcing others to do one's bidding, the man finds himself losing every battle until he finally discovers the chair's inner longing. The parable is slight, the effects unevenly achieved, but they leave the door open for others to experiment along these and similar lines.

The man is filmed at times in frame-by-frame animation, in what McLaren has called the "pixillation" technique; at other times, he is merely speeded up by a slower filming process. The chair is maneuvered by hidden strings in the hands of Evelyn Lambert.

Two Bagatelles (3 minutes, color)
Produced by the National Film Board of Canada in 1952

Two Bagatelles is made up of two brief exercises filmed in a lighthearted mood in preparation for McLaren's deadly serious *Neighbors*. "On the Lawn," the first bagatelle, is a short waltz set to McLaren's own synthetic music, in which animator Grant Munro skates effortlessly on the grass without moving his feet, and then whirls faster and faster in a circle while sitting down. "In the Backyard," set to old-fashioned calliope music, has Munro slipping up and down a ladder, sliding on his back with feet up in the air, and changing clothes every few seconds. The dancing titles at the beginning and end of the film are as endearing as any you will ever see anywhere.

Neighbors (9 minutes, color)
Directed by Norman McLaren; photographed by Wolf Koenig
Enacted by animators Jean-Paul Ladouceur and Grant Munro
Produced by the National Film Board of Canada in 1952

This hard-hitting parable on the futility of violence and war is
one of the rare and outstanding examples of humorous animation techniques used for totally serious purposes. The pixillation
techniques in *Two Bagatelles* begin here in an equally amusing
way, as two neighbors dispute the ownership of a wildflower.
But by the end of the film these same techniques are used to
intensify the beastlike madness of the two "neighbors."

A number of other fantasy effects are put to excellent use:
cardboard house-fronts stand side-by-side in a real landscape;
the two men dance in mid-air and skate effortlessly on the
lawn; the picket fence plants itself into the ground, and later
provides makeshift swords for hand-to-hand combat between
the men. In the final merciless battle, the faces of the two men
are altered in a swift series of flashes until they become in-
human monsters. The film ends as two flowers pop up and
entwine themselves around the neighboring graves of the two
men. The moral, says McLaren in the fast-flashing multi-lingual
titles at the end of the film, is simply: "Love Thy Neighbor."
Certainly no other film style could state the message in so
condensed, persuasive, and haunting a way as *Neighbors* does.

119

Blinkity Blank (6 minutes, color)
Made by Norman McLaren, at the National Film Board of
Canada, in 1955
Music by Maurice Blackburn

Blinkity Blank is so difficult a film to describe that perhaps it
is best to tell only how it was made. Using a simple penknife,
a sewing needle, and a razor blade, McLaren engraved individual figures and designs directly on to 35mm black emulsion-
coated film and then colored each frame by hand with trans-
parent cellulose dyes and a sable-hair brush.

Movement from frame to frame is not continuous in the usual
sense, but intermittent—creating a strange effect of things
popping out of nowhere every now and then. "Optically most
of the film consists of nothing," McLaren has written. "I en-
grave a frame here and a frame there, leaving many frames
untouched and blank, sprinkling, as it were, the images on the
empty hand of time; but sprinkling carefully—in relation to each
other, to the spaces between, to the music, and to the idea that
emerged as I drew."

The film is peopled with sweet and sour monsters, with hens
and eggs (with Russian Easter decorations). There are many
fabulous transformations, sometimes too quick for the eye to
recognize or the brain to remember. The film is based on the
laws of persistence of vision. "If the film does not succeed,"
McLaren has said, "it is partly because I have not yet fully
understood those laws."

Canon (9 minutes, color)
Made by Norman McLaren and Grant Munro
Music composed by Eldon Rathburn
Produced by the National Film Board of Canada in 1965

Music sustains the visual form and movement in this illustration of three different types of musical canons with three different types of animation. The first is done with simple *ABCD* blocks as they move and turn to a canon version of "Frère Jacques." The second, animated by Grant Munro, involves two little cut-out men who bounce and swing to a simple two-part canon, in precise yet carefree style.

The third, however, is the one that surprises and delights beyond measure. Here Grant Munro appears on screen, dressed in a silly get-up; he hops, turns, bows, and kicks as his image repeats itself on the screen to accompany each added voice of the music. The pictures and music are exact and humorous, carrying instruction and relaxation to their highest potentials. *Canon* is a film to enjoy on many levels—from the ridiculous to the sublime.

121

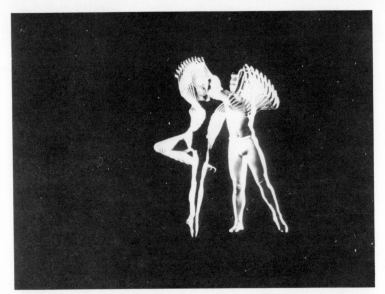

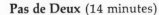

Pas de Deux (14 minutes)
Directed by Norman McLaren; choreography by Ludmilla Chiraieff
Music arranged by Maurice Blackburn
Produced by the National Film Board of Canada in 1969

Pas de Deux is a multiple-image, live-action film strongly reminiscent of Dr. Marey's Chronophotographe pictures—and of some moments of Len Lye's brilliant *Rainbow Dance*.

Against a black background, the intensely highlighted bodies of a male and a female dancer are filmed first in normal photographic style; then, as the images begin to multiply, an increasingly abstract effect is achieved. The sense of recognition is maintained by having each set of multiple images revert to normal, in most instances, before going on to the next set.

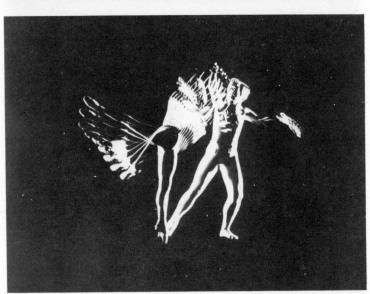

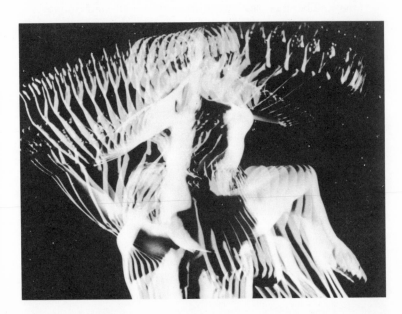

The ballet movements were multiplied in the printing process, McLaren has explained, permitting technology to do the work that he often has elected to do by hand. But the opening out and closing in of the images, and their arrangement in constantly revealing patterns, has rested on the filmmaker's personal judgment. "An immediate classic," one reviewer has called the film. "One of the most beautiful dance films ever made," said another. Certainly the marriage of reality and fantasy has never been more thrillingly consummated than in *Pas de Deux*.

These are a few samples of McLaren's prodigious body of work. The film world must forever be indebted to the National Film Board of Canada for being the first to adopt and sustain a film artist for the greater part of his career. What another gifted animator might have accomplished in McLaren's place cannot be surmised, but we are safe in saying that the world of animation has derived immeasurable benefits from McLaren's enviable productivity, curiosity, humanity, and artistry.

McLaren's place in an overview of film history is perhaps not among animators, but rather with the great film illusionists of all times—with Méliès and Chaplin. Like their films, everything he has created is worth seeing, although each work has its own individual merit and its own ups and downs. For in McLaren's films, as in the films of Méliès and Chaplin, we begin to understand the words of the psychologist Alfred Adler, who once said: "Everything that moves has a soul!"

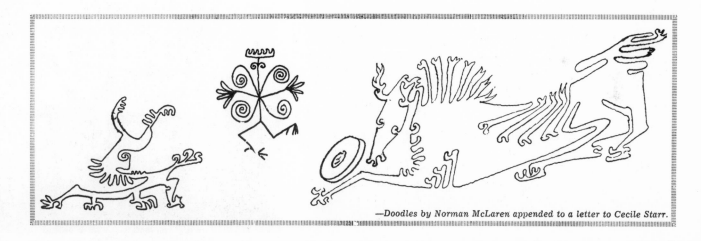

—Doodles by Norman McLaren appended to a letter to Cecile Starr.

Fantasy and Reality: A Conclusion

Every introduction must end somewhere. This book ends with an exploration of some of the techniques that combine fantasy and reality in the experimental film (which, in turn, are greatly influencing the contemporary feature film).

FILMS BY HILARY HARRIS

Longhorns (6 minutes, 1951) goes back to Marcel Duchamp's turntable to provide the basic movement of horns rotating in space against a natural background of grass, trees, and sky. The camera moves gracefully and freely to compound motion within motion in this simple, yet often hypnotic, film exercise.

Generation (3 minutes, color, 1956) is a visual kaleidoscope of color, form, and movement, combined with Harris' unusual emphatic and repetitive musical effects. John Grierson has interpreted the film as "the making and the growing and the building of all things—the heart of life." (See pictures on page 127.)

Highway (6 minutes, color, 1968) has been expertly described by an unusually articulate eighth-grader, after one viewing:

> The film was in 3 parts. The first was in the afternoon or mid-day, the second in the evening and at night, the third in the morning. The subject was roads, cars, underpasses, highways. They were abstracted by techniques into interesting patterns of dark, light, and movement. One of the best shots in my opinion was of underpasses very quickly shooting back and forth. Another was in the second part at night of lights and traffic. They were so abstracted that they became moving lights on a dark field. Visually the film was good—the quickness of the succession of shots was very exciting. At the end pull-backs and zoom-in close-ups were used for the first time on traffic and traffic-signs, while the tempo of the film speeded up to a climax and then ended.

Donn Pennebaker's *Daybreak Express*

Jerome Hill's *Canaries*

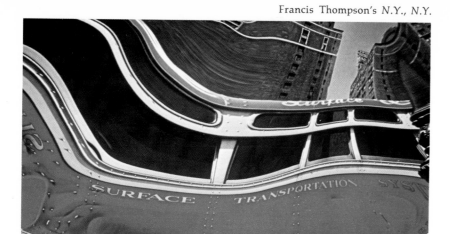

Francis Thompson's *N.Y., N.Y.*

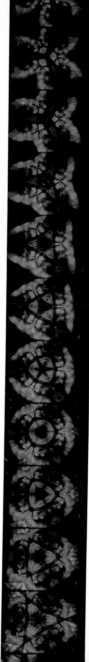

Above and left:
Hilary Harris's *Generation*

In the Street (16 minutes, silent; a piano score by Arthur Kleiner
is available on a long-play record)
Photographed by Helen Levitt, James Agee, and Janice Loeb;
edited by Helen Levitt

Although the film was photographed in the late 1940s and early
1950s, its vision of the real slum world is suspended somewhere between the timeliness and the otherworldliness of reality
and fantasy. An introductory title announces that for the poor
the street is both a theater and a battleground. The street
shown here is in New York City's East Harlem.

At the start of the film, people walk and look, gesture and
talk, generally unaware that they are being photographed. Then
images begin to recur: a child presses his tongue against a
window, young girls dance together in the street, children appear in Halloween masks and costumes, boys sling chalk bags
at each other. As the film ends, the street children peer into
the camera, make faces, and thus remind us that what we saw
earlier is rarely seen by the camera, or by the human eye for
that matter. As in Helen Levitt's still photographs, an almost
miraculous spirit hovers around the people, particularly the
young people, in the film.

The Canaries (4 minutes, color)
Directed and edited by Jerome Hill in 1968

Vivid memories of Méliès' hand-colored films prompted Jerome Hill to apply color by hand to short films. Painting directly on color negative meant that opposite coloration had to be used: green would develop as red, and so forth. Using this technique, he has been able to add pictures of sounds, feelings, and other presences.

In some shots the filmmaker achieves subliminal effects by painting alternate frames in contrasting colors, which gives an odd vibrating sensation. Hill has written that there seems no limit to the plasticity of this technique, but he admits that it is a serious strain on the eyes. "I have tried magnifying lenses, Polaroid glasses, all sort of sight-preserving devices," he has written, "but find myself continually returning to a 15-minute-on and 15-minute-off routine—with closed eyes in the rest periods. Even with this, my prescription has had to be changed!" (See color pictures on page 126.)

N.Y., N.Y. (15 minutes, color)
Photographed by Francis Thompson in the 1940s and 1950s; edited and released in 1961; music by Gene Forrell

N.Y., N.Y. is a documentary fantasy about life in a very crowded city, seen through various photographic distortion techniques. "I wanted to make fun, in a new way, of the ridiculousness of the life of a New Yorker," filmmaker Francis Thompson has recalled. Realistically, the film follows a recognizable chronology from morning to night; even a number of its distorted images are those we might see reflected in an automobile headlight or a rain puddle. Fantastically, it conveys the abstract monotony, the intriguing beauty, and the inane futility of city life in its use of distorting lenses, multiple-printing, and high-speed shooting of individual sequences. (See color pictures on page 127.)

Francis Thompson, at first a student of painting, began using a movie camera in 1935 to capture the feeling of New York City's architecture. While he was filming one day on top of an open Fifth Avenue double-decker bus, his shots blurred because of improper threading. Like Méliès, he stumbled by accident upon a technique that led to many others. The footage for *N.Y., N.Y.* took nearly two decades to complete; it was shot for the most part on the busman's holiday weekends that Thompson took after his regular week's work as a documentary film director.

Daybreak Express (5 minutes, color)
Photographed and edited by Donn Pennebaker in 1953

This impressionistic film journey in and alongside an elevated/subway train opens and closes realistically, with natural sounds punctuating the visual elements. The middle sequences, which make up the bulk of the film, use natural and artificial distortions to plunge us into a world of fantasy, rhythmically edited to the music of Duke Ellington. Lights flashing between moving cars, convoluted patterns of a bridge performing a wild and intricate dance, buildings bulging at their seams—these are only a few of the film's vivid images. Then, as the music slows down and disappears entirely, the pictures and sounds return us to the world of dismal reality. (See color picture on page 126.)

But we should not forget that even this reality is an illusion. "The only reality you have in the movie theater," Hans Richter has pointed out, "is the screen."

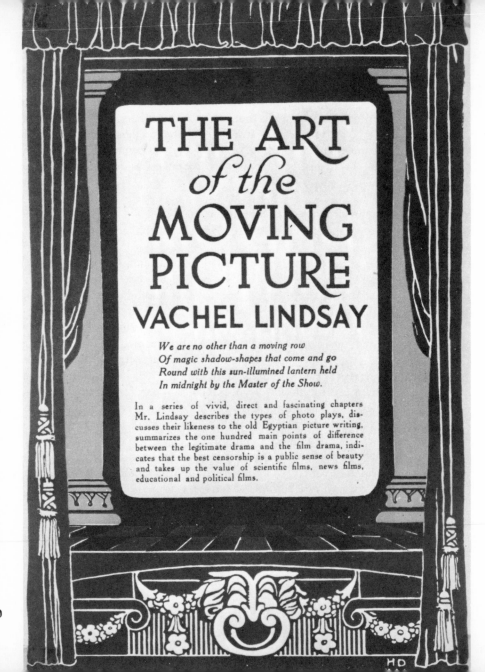

THE ART
of the
MOVING PICTURE
VACHEL LINDSAY

We are no other than a moving row
Of magic shadow-shapes that come and go
Round with this sun-illumined lantern held
In midnight by the Master of the Show.

In a series of vivid, direct and fascinating chapters Mr. Lindsay describes the types of photo plays, discusses their likeness to the old Egyptian picture writing, summarizes the one hundred main points of difference between the legitimate drama and the film drama, indicates that the best censorship is a public sense of beauty and takes up the value of scientific films, news films, educational and political films.

Film Study in the Classroom

Notes for Teachers and Students

Students in high school, junior high, and even grade school, I am convinced, can easily learn almost everything about film essentials that college students often have to be badgered into learning. Young minds are open and flexible. Young students use their eyes and ears more directly. And they clearly enjoy looking at new kinds of films they never dreamed existed. "Why don't they show films like this on TV?" one seventh-grader asked after seeing his first Méliès film. "Can we see it over again?" an enthusiastic group of fifth-graders asked after seeing McLaren's *Le Merle*.

Questions of this kind have constantly sustained my feeling that we were on the right track. But the right track for me may not be everyone else's right track. This book has been written in the hope that I can share my own teaching and learning experiences with those teachers and students who are starting out in film study, or who are not entirely pleased with the start they already have made.

No book can supply all the answers to how to teach a course in anything—but it is my hope that some of my hints and suggestions can be adapted for other situations and needs. I should like to add that although I have worked with film in many different capacities, it is only as a teacher that I have learned anything significant about the subject.

The following notes are intended to answer some of the questions that may arise when teachers and students are using this book in the classroom:

1. *Learning to See*. Increasing our ability to see is one of the most rewarding results of this approach to film study. Young students often see and hear better than their teachers, for the older and the more educated we become, the less likely it is that we can use our senses creatively, or even accurately. Giving the students this advantage over their teacher seems to me by no means unhealthy. It helps restore some balance to the classroom, which almost always places the teacher in a super-human position and in turn can make learning difficult for many students and impossible for others.

2. *Analyzing Film*. No student or teacher can see or remember or put into words all the elements that are present in even the simplest film, but everyone in the class can make one or two interesting observations. I have found it productive to ask individual students to look for some specific element, rather than to take on the film as a whole. In showing a Chaplin film, for example, I may ask them to find ways in which Chaplin moves the different parts of his body expressively—eyes, mouth, nose, head, shoulders, feet, or even his rear end.

With an intricate film like *Night Mail*, I may ask each student to take mental or written notes on one shot of his own choosing. After the film is shown, as each student describes the shot he has selected, we get a fairly good composite of the film's various elements.

3. *Right and Wrong*. Film teachers and students have to be wrong, at least some of the time, about what they remember from a given shot or sequence. Such inaccuracies are part of the illusory nature of film itself. If we linger too long over the specifics of any one shot, we lose its overall suggestive effect within the sequence or the entire film. On the other hand, if we deal only with its suggestive effect, we lose sight of the specific elements that create the effect. A balance between the two is the most desirable goal.

4. *Putting Imagination to Work*. The more imaginative the film, the more imaginative our approach to it can be. Before showing *Rain*, a teacher may ask the students to imagine how they would make a film of that title, what they would stress, and how they would organize the material. When they watch the film, they are then more likely to be attentive to its content and construction than they would have been without this imaginative exercise.

The value of music can be experimented with by showing a silent film like H_2O several times, with a different musical recording or tape for each screening.

Imagining how Méliès might have made a film called *Nanook of the North* can re-enforce the students' memories as well as their imaginations.

5. *Early Short Films*. I stress early short movies because I have found them fun in the classroom, and remarkably easy to learn from. Their brevity makes them appropriate for the average 45-minute class period, with time remaining for discussion or a second viewing, if desired—or possibly for another short film. Short films are easier to assimilate than long ones, and they seem ideally suited to young students. When I occasionally show a long film to a class below college level— *Nanook of the North*, for example—I usually stop the projector after the first few minutes to discuss the specifics of style and content in just these opening sequences. Otherwise the class tends to get too involved in the story, and in their own emotional reactions, for a really valuable discussion.

Young filmmakers particularly seem to benefit from seeing a variety of early films whose general limitations (short running time, small budget, limited equipment and resources, and pantomimed actions) often resemble their own first productions. Inversely, students who have not had a chance to see film language develop, with their own eyes, are often seriously disadvantaged in their growth as filmmakers. Old movies are also a delightful link with the past. Many students are sur-

prised to discover that humor and love and mischief existed as far back as seventy years ago. New films are certainly not to be ignored, but I have always found them more interesting if students are already familiar with the early film traditions.

6. *Selecting Films for Study*. The importance of carefully selecting and arranging the films for classroom showing cannot be stressed too strongly. Random showings generally lead to random learning. A meaningful succession of films gives the eye and mind a firm basis upon which the natural learning process can build.

Anyone who sees in succession Lumière's train entering the station, then Porter's *Great Train Robbery*, followed by Griffith's *Lonedale Operator*, does not have to be taught how the story film developed. It is already imprinted, in living images, on his mind. Of course he will need assistance in articulating what he has seen, through talking and writing about the films. If several weeks are devoted to the chronological development of the early film, several other classes can deal with the films of individual artists—Charlie Chaplin, whom, as one student wrote, "you can't beat," or Norman McLaren, who has generally been a favorite with most of my young students. Different styles of European avant-garde films can be sampled, or the teacher and students may want to select a group of films dealing with contemporary techniques and subjects.

7. *Comparisons are Helpful*. Students often see and remember more accurately if they have seen other films of similar or contrasting styles. *An Occurrence at Owl Creek Bridge*, for example, is a more rewarding learning experience if it is shown before or after the two earlier versions.

An individual artist's talents and growth can be assessed in the selection of several films by one filmmaker—Hilary Harris, for example, or the animator Carmen D'Avino. Excerpts from Hollywood films can show the disparities and similarities in "film language" among widely recognized directors. Other groupings can be developed by teachers and students to suit their own interests, and can be changed and rearranged from year to year.

8. *Film Discussion in the Classroom.* In group discussion of a film, it is advisable to concentrate as much as possible on what is actually on the screen, rather than on any general and abstract topic. It is usually better, for example, to discuss how Chaplin gives a specific gesture a recognizable meaning and feeling all its own, rather than to take on the broad topic of "Man against Machine" or "The Relationship of the Individual to Society."

Film is specific and concrete; the closer we stay in our discussions to these concrete specifics the more positive the classroom learning is likely to be. The excerpted sequences from *Intruder in the Dust* might produce a heated, even effective, discussion of the condition of the black man in society today, but in most cases I have found it far more productive to discuss something we have all seen—how the black-and-white relationship is presented visually by the camera, for example. The feelings that these images evoke can then be more generally shared and understood.

9. *Classroom Criticism.* As we study films more closely, we see that all of them have defects. Alexander Alexeieff once told me that for him great works have great defects, mediocre works have mediocre defects, and dull works have dull defects. When I was teaching at Columbia University, many beginning film-makers brought me their films, which inevitably were full of weaknesses. I eventually classified them into two groups: those whose defects were original and promising, and those whose defects were imitative and lifeless. Often it seemed that students who were first and loudest in denouncing other people's shortcomings were slowest in seeing their own. Generally a class is happier and more productive focusing on a film's achievements rather than dwelling on its defects.

10. *"I Liked It . . . I Didn't Like It."* Often I have had to interrupt a seemingly endless tug-of-war of opinions about a film by reminding the participants that when they say they did or did not like it, the *it* is what we want to know more about. Just what did each spectator see that was appealing or unappealing to him? (See "The Audience is Part of the Film," by Tom Daly, for an enlargement of this attitude—page 138.) The more unusual a film is, the more varied we can expect the class reactions to be. Francis Thompson's *N.Y., N.Y.*, for example, evoked this range of responses from eighth-graders in several New York City public schools:

Pro:	Con:
"The use of lenses in this film was absolutely fantastic. It gave the appearance that one subject was really five or six. The film was like a story which many people did not realize . . ."	"The whole picture was utter confusion, and it was like moving op-art. The film was pleasant and attracted the eye, but for aims or for the mind, forget it."
"The film is truly a credit to the imagination of the film-maker, whose honor it is to have composed such an excellent film . . ."	"I thought this particular film was very boring and most of the time it hurt my eyes to look at it. I found this to be very monotonous because buildings were always used."
"The shots were all distorted in one fashion or another but were always constantly changing. The colors melted in with the shapes and produced an exciting mixture . . ."	"I didn't think it was too well made, since they just showed the strange effects of that kind of camera, although it was a very good idea."

11. *Film Study in Art, English, and Social Studies Classes.* Since film study rarely is offered as a separate course in high schools or lower grades, it is often included in classes in art, English and drama, or social studies and communications. Art teachers are most likely to enjoy a study of avant-garde films, animation, and other kinds of fantasy films. English and drama classes can benefit from a thorough study of the fiction film, and they may find all types of film valuable in stimulating the reading of related short stories, plays, poems, and novels, as well as in creative writing.

Social studies, history, and communications classes can draw upon innumerable documentary and historical re-enactment films, which hopefully will help awaken an interest in the past for students who have not yet responded to written material.

All classes will benefit from discovering how film began, how a story is told in film, and how reality can be dramatized or fantasized. However useful film may be as a stimulus in other areas, it can also be profitably studied for its own sake.

12. *Tests and Grades.* Classroom tests are most useful if they help students see how much they are learning and how pleasant learning is. One test I enjoy giving a class is to show two or three minutes of a film and ask the students to write down what they saw, or to write an imagined description of the rest of the film.

If film study is not offered as a separate course, grades may not be necessary. If grades are given, I try to base them on each student's actual progress in the class, rather than on the level at which the student began. This offers an opportunity for students who have been slow or backward in their regular subjects to advance without self-consciousness or fear.

13. *The Teacher is Part of the Class.* Partly to keep awake, and partly to set a learning tone for the class, the teacher must constantly look at the films and learn. In every outstanding film there is always something new to see and think about. And with

so many good films to choose from, the film teacher can include a few he or she hasn't seen recently, or at all—a new Méliès, perhaps, or a different Griffith.

The teacher should also try doing a written assignment once in a while. It's surprising how difficult it is to find time to write even the easiest and shortest paper!

14. *How to Obtain Films.* It is awkward and time-consuming to rely on major film outlets, located in New York, Chicago, or California, unless you are situated in these areas. Preferably your school or school system should include a basic selection of film-study films in its regular film library. There may also be a good 16mm film collection in a nearby college or university, from which you may rent some of the films you need.

It may be helpful to join ranks with other teachers who can also use the films you want: *Le Merle,* for example, is fine for French classes, and *Canon* should send music classes into ecstasy.

15. *Silent Film Speeds.* Since many of the films I recommend are silent, it's desirable to have a projector that runs at both silent (16 frames per second) and sound (24 per second) speeds. Even better is a projector with an adjustable range between the two, since many silent films were originally shot at irregular speeds. It pays to keep adjusting the speed, even within a given film, slowing it down when the action seems too fast, speeding it up when the timing is too slow or flickering.

Incidentally, from fifth grade up it should always be possible to entrust the projection to one or more students who really understand the machine, and who in turn can teach the rudiments of its operation to other students. It is usually awkward to be leading the class and running the projector at the same time—and it's good for the students to take over this responsibility. One warning, however: they should constantly be reminded that projectors and films are valuable and fragile—and must be treated accordingly.

16. *Film Terminology*. Long shot, moving camera, close-up—unless these abstract terms name something specific, they are of little use in film study. If we say, however, "the camera moves to show the robbers running down the hill," or "the long shot of Chaplin sitting at the rear of the rink," or "the close-up of the monkey wrench"—these film terms can be understood by almost everyone.

Still, if a glossary is needed, there is a fairly complete one in Ernest Lindgren's *The Art of the Film* (New York: Macmillan, 1970), a book that can also be recommended for its basic approach to film.

In connection with film terminology, let me add that I think it is a mistake to refer to camera or editing "tricks" as though there were something false or deceptive in their use. Tricks they may be, but they are the tricks of the filmmaker's trade and art —as essential to him as colors are to a painter, or sound to a musician.

17. *Does Film Study Destroy the Young Filmmaker's Creativity?* It might be argued that this is so, if students began their filmmaking with relatively little exposure to film. But today's film students have already been immeasurably, and usually unconsciously, influenced by an almost incessant flow of cartoons, serials, and commercials on the home television set, not to mention their added moviegoing experiences in the theater. It seems to me that the classroom is the ideal place to offer them the counter-influences of such fresh and original films as those created by a Méliès, a Richter, or a McLaren. The goal should be to help broaden students' taste and interests as much as possible.

18. *Does Study Spoil the Fun of Movies?* In my eighteen years of film teaching, I have never found it so. There are times when students wonder whether they will ever again relax and just enjoy what they see on the screen. But this is a temporary state, and before long they are enjoying all sorts of movies as much as they ever did, or even more. When they find a film dull, they have the added fun of understanding why it doesn't work for them.

In the interim period, I have sometimes read this Zen poem as a reassurance:

To the man who knows nothing,
mountains are mountains,
waters are waters,
and trees are trees.

But when he has studied and knows a little,
mountains are no longer mountains,
water is no longer water,
and trees are no longer trees.

But when he has thoroughly understood,
mountains are once again mountains,
waters are waters,
and trees are trees.

Study Notes

Foreword

The expanded 1922 edition of Vachel Lindsay's *Art of the Moving Picture* has been reprinted in hardcover and paperback editions (New York: Liveright, 1970). Despite its unwieldy thesis—that different types of movies correspond to the different arts—the book is decidedly worthwhile. Several chapters are included in various anthologies.

What is a Motion Picture?

The chapter entitled "Imagination," in Welford Beaton's *Know Your Movies* (Hollywood: Howard Hill, 1932) is recommended to anyone who can find this little-known and long out-of-print volume. The quotation from Ingmar Bergman first appeared in an interview in *Cahiers du Cinéma* (July 1956); it has appeared in several anthologies, in different translations.

How the Movies Began

Kenneth MacGowan's *Behind the Screen: The History and Technique of the Motion Picture* (New York: Delacorte Press, 1965) contains fine illustrations and an excellent summary of the pre-camera and early motion-picture devices.

An illustrated booklet entitled *The Origins of the Motion Picture*, by David B. Thomas, is available for under $1.00 from the British Information Services, 845 Third Avenue, New York, New York 10022.

C. W. Ceram's *Archeology of the Cinema* (New York: Harcourt Brace Jovanovich, 1965) has exceptionally fine illustrations of this period.

Film: Animated Cartoons: The Toy That Grew Up (18 minutes), directed by Roger Leenhardt in 1947, is still the best film showing these pre-camera devices in action; it is available for 16mm rental and purchase from Film Images, 17 West 60th Street, New York, New York 10023.

Projects: Art teachers should have no difficulty in providing materials and ideas for student-made thaumatropes, flip-books (best made on 3x5 index cards), zoetropes, and other persistence-of-vision toys.

Very young students may enjoy the zoetrope-like Magic Mirror Movies which can be played and shown on any 78 rpm phonograph and are available at a reasonable price from Magic Mirror Movie Company, 59 Grove Street, New Canaan, Connecticut 06840.

Other moving-picture toys appear on the market now and again, and it's best to buy a supply as soon as you see them, because often they disappear almost immediately.

Photographs in Motion

Muybridge's *Animals in Motion* and *The Human Figure in Motion* (New York: Dover, 1955) are used today throughout the world by artists and students; most of the human figures are photographed nude. (*Note:* If nudity is not a problem, see David Hanson's delightful two-minute color film, *Homage to Muybridge,* made in 1965 and available for 16mm rental and purchase from the University of Southern California, Division of Cinema, Film Distribution Section, University Park, Los Angeles, California 90007.)

Terry Ramsay's *A Million and One Nights*, originally published in 1926 (New York: Simon and Schuster, 1964), is an anecdotal and at times fictitious account of the early struggles to control the movie industry.

Lewis Jacobs' *The Rise of the American Film* (New York: Teachers College Press, 1967) is a reprint of his 1939 volume, with an added essay on the experimental film in America for the years 1921-47.

Films: The Biography of the Motion Picture Camera (22 minutes), also directed by Roger Leenhardt in 1947, is highly recommended and is available for 16mm rental and purchase from Film Images, 17 West 60th Street, New York, New York 10023.

Origins of the Motion Picture (20 minutes), produced by the U.S. Navy, has some fine footage, but the approach is didactic and lifeless. Available for 16mm rental from the Museum of Modern Art Film Library, 11 West 53rd Street, New York, New York 10019; also from the New York University Film Library, 26 Washington Place, New York, New York 10003, and from other university film libraries.

A program of early Lumière films, covering the early 1895-6 programs, is available for 16mm rental from the Museum of Modern Art Film Library and from Film Images (addresses above).

The Great Méliès (pronounced *May-lee-ace'*)

The Méliès chapter in Lewis Jacobs' *The Rise of the American Film* is the best English-language introduction to Méliès to date.

Georges Méliès, by Georges Sadoul (Paris Éditions Seghers, 1961), is currently available only in French and can be purchased from special film bookshops.

Films: Every Méliès film is a special for Méliès fans like myself. Blackhawk Films, 1235 West Fifth Street, Davenport, Iowa 52808, has a growing selection available for 16mm, 8mm, and Super-8 purchase, at moderate prices; the prints, however, are of uneven quality. There is also the problem of the seemingly endless titles that precede each film; I can only suggest that you cut them out and splice the films back together again.

Using four stars as highest rating, and one star as worth seeing once, here is my list of my favorite Méliès combination reels available from Blackhawk:

***La Fantaisie de Méliès* (includes ****Extraordinary Illusions,
       *The Enchanted Well, and ***The Apparition)
**The Magic of Méliès* (includes **Jupiter's Thunderbolts,
       ***The Mermaid, and ***The Magic Lantern)
**The Surrealism of Méliès* (includes *The Ballet Master's
       Dream and **The Kingdom of the Fairies)
**La Comédie et Magique de Méliès* (includes *The Witch's
       Revenge and ***The Inn Where No Man Rests)

Note: The reels listed above are of 1903-4 vintage and have been copied from the Library of Congress Paper Print Collection in Washington D. C.

The Museum of Modern Art Film Library's 65-minute program (****A Trip to the Moon, ****Conquest of the Pole, *The Palace of the Arabian Nights and **The Doctor's Secret, along with a half-minute film entitled ***The Conjurer) is entirely too long and exhausting to be viewed at one sitting. In general the Museum's prints are excellent. *A Trip to the Moon* and *Conquest of the Pole* can be rented individually from the Museum (educational groups only) and from several other 16mm libraries across the country. In some cases 16mm prints are also for sale; check and compare prices and print quality before buying.

***Méliès' Color Films*, a combination reel that includes ****An Astronomer's Dream, a short version of ****A Trip to The Moon (in which the rocket lands in the moon's mouth, not in its eye), and ***An Oriental Fantasy, can be rented from CCM Films, 866 Third Avenue, New York, New York 10022.

***Le Grand Méliès* (30 minutes) is available in French, without English subtitles, for 16mm rental only to educational groups from the French-American Cultural Services, 972 Fifth Avenue, New York, New York 10021. It was directed by Georges Franju and features Méliès' widow, son, and grandson in a fascinating re-enactment of his life. Included are ***The Vanishing Lady, ***The Man with the Rubber Head, ****The Melomaniac, and excerpts from ****A Trip to the Moon, all in fine condition.

Special Notes on Méliès and his Films

I showed *A Trip to the Moon* one year in the opening session of a film class of seventh-graders, and I found them so excited by it that we made a project of screening every Méliès film we could find. This totalled a dozen or so little films (and by now there are more), from which we could see how Méliès repeated himself from time to time, how the tricks could work marvelously well in some instances and could fail to delight us in others. We laughed at his good humor, marvelled at his imaginative devices, wondered how he filmed many of his sensational effects and why so few are attempted today. In short, we came to "know" Georges Méliès.

Some students read about Méliès in Lewis Jacobs' *The Rise of the American Film,* and several wrote reports about what they had read.

The students wrote comments of their own:

"The film I learned the most from was *A Trip to the Moon.* It used actual staging and cartoon-type backdrops . . . It taught me how this could combine and how if not having the materials one could make a film."

". . . by observing similar characteristics of films of Méliès, I noticed what ideas made up his style and what he did with the things he had to work with. All of the filmmakers whose films we studied in detail had their own limitations, but not to the extent of Méliès."

Not everyone "liked" the Méliès films, and some could give their reasons:

"His techniques seem crude and the good magic tricks he plays are often swallowed up in an elaborate crowd scene."

"The repetition of a constant long shot had somewhat of a dull and boring influence upon the audience; however, the eye-catching magical acts overshadowed this for the most part."

After seeing *Le Grand Méliès,* many students were crushed to find the great Méliès selling toys in his old age. We discussed the fact that many famous artists have died impoverished and forgotten (while businessmen seldom do). It was a valuable lesson in distinguishing the roles of the creative artist and the acquisitive financier.

Several students wrote their own short scenarios in the style of Méliès, using titles of films now lost to us: *Smarter Than the Teacher, A Janitor in Trouble, The Mysterious Paper, Addition and Subtraction, The Triple Lady, The Snow Man.*

Nearly everyone in the class did something, either on his own or working with one or two other students. We collected their papers, and some of my own notes, in a loose-leaf notebook, which remained in class, so anyone could look through when he wished. I did not give grades for their written work, nor did I check to see that everyone had written something.

Everyone learned. Some learned quicker and more than others. But a class is not an assembly line. It's more like a symphony orchestra. Each person makes his own contribution to the whole; some are virtuoso soloists, others play the tambourine or clang the cymbals—but all are important and necessary to a rich musical assembly. In the classroom, if each student can work harmoniously with the others, no matter how large or how small his role may be, everything is going well. Of course we hope that each student will increase his abilities, and we encourage him to—but we gain nothing by pushing him beyond his actual capacities.

The Méliès films made deep and lasting impressions on us all. They were powerful and original images, and we felt that we ourselves had discovered them. To retain this sense of discovery, and to build upon it, is the film teacher's greatest challenge. In most other subjects the teacher is far too pressured to experiment with new types of learning. In film study there is no need for such pressure, and when we are dealing with youngsters who have difficulties with traditional learning techniques, we can be as open-minded and as creative as we like.

Film may perhaps open new doors to learning. Just as we recognize the uniqueness and the limitations of so great an artist as Méliès, why not also recognize the uniqueness of each student in the class, his right to his own opinions, his limitations, and his strengths?

* * *

Telling a Story in Pictures

The Tolstoy quotation appears in Appendix 3 of Jay Leyda's *Kino: A History of the Russian and Soviet Film* (New York: Macmillan, 1960). The book is a scholarly work, of which only the opening chapters are appropriate to an introductory study of film.

James Agee's collected film reviews and articles, entitled *Agee on Film* (New York: McDowell, Oblensky, 1958), include his extraordinary and widely quoted tribute to D. W. Griffith.

E. M. Forster's *Aspects of the Novel* (New York: Harcourt Brace, 1927) has pointed out to me many ways in which the fiction film can be better understood.

For a detailed analysis of *The Great Train Robbery,* including a full scenario taken from the 1904 Edison catalogue, see Lewis Jacobs' *The Rise of the American Film,* pp. 35-51.

The review of *Rescued from an Eagle's Nest* appeared in *Motion Picture World* on February 1, 1908.

Films: The Great Train Robbery and *Rescued from an Eagle's Nest* are both available for 16mm, 8mm, and Super-8 purchase from Blackhawk Films, 1235 West Fifth Street, Davenport, Iowa 52808. They can be rented on 16mm from the Museum of Modern Art Film Library, 11 West 53rd Street, New York, New York 10019 (educational groups only)—and from other 16mm libraries.

D. W. Griffith

He achieved what no other known man has ever achieved. To watch his work is like being witness to the beginning of melody, or the . . . emergence, coordination, and first eloquence of language, the birth of an art: and to realize that this is all the work of one man.

—James Agee, in *Agee on Film*

The Lillian Gish quotation first appeared in "D. W. Griffith: A Great American," (*Harper's Bazaar,* October 1940). Miss Gish's *The Movies, Mr. Griffith and Me* (New York: Prentice Hall, 1969) looks back over her early years in the movies, and pays a warm tribute to the "master," D. W. Griffith.

When the Movies Were Young (New York: E. P. Dutton, 1925; republished and slightly amended in 1969) by Linda Arvidson, then Mrs. D. W. Griffith, is pleasant reading.

Chapter VII of Lewis Jacobs' *The Rise of the American Film,* which is entitled "D. W. Griffith: New Discoveries," is highly recommended for use in introductory film studies.

Robert M. Henderson's *D. W. Griffith: The Years at Biograph* (New York: Farrar, Straus and Giroux, 1970) is useful for some specific details and facts about this period in Griffith's career.

D. W. Griffith, American Film Master, by Iris Barry, with an annotated feature film list by Eileen Bowser (New York: Museum of Modern Art, 1965), is readable, condensed, and well illustrated.

Films: The Lonedale Operator is available for purchase from Blackhawk Films, 1235 West Fifth Street, Davenport, Iowa 52808, on 16mm, 8mm, and Super-8—but you have to edit out those printed titles at the beginning, and sometimes in the middle, of the films. *The New York Hat* is available from Blackhawk, but only on 8mm and Super-8. Other recommended Griffith short films, available from Blackhawk, are: ****The Musketeers of Pig Alley (1912), ****The Battle at Elderbush Gulch (1913), ***The Lonely Villa (1909), **The Battle (1911—incidentally, one of Vachel Lindsay's favorites), and ***Enoch Arden (but beware the 16mm sound version, with a narrator reading the poem as accompaniment to the filmed story!).

The Museum of Modern Art Film Library, 11 West 53rd Street, New York, New York, 10019, also rents *The Lonedale Operator* on 16mm, to educational groups only. I do not recommend showing Griffith's long films to beginning students, as fine and important as they are. Incidentally, the script of *The New York Hat* was written by Anita Loos, when she was a teen-age schoolgirl.

The Magic of the Movies

My ideas about physical, emotional, and intellectual responses to the movies derive largely from a talk given by Tom Daly some years ago to the Toronto Film Study Group. I have shortened it to exclude specific references to Eisenstein's *The General Line*, the film under discussion on that occasion, since it is not a film for beginners. A summary of Daly's talk was printed in *Canadian Newsreel*, August 1954, from which this version has been edited.

"The Audience is Part of the Film"
by Tom Daly
Executive Producer, National Film Board of Canada

In discussing films and criticizing them, we always tend to talk about the picture and the maker of the picture, and forget what is involved in the reactions of the people in the audience —that is, ourselves. We take it for granted that there is only one film in question—up there on the screen—and that we are all equally absorbing it. We forget that the film is only a "thing," a piece of celluloid, a matter of physics and chemistry, until it is completed by making contact with the members of the audience. When anyone afterwards speaks of "the film," he really speaks only of the flow of impressions and reactions *he* experienced. Probably no one is capable of experiencing "the whole film." Each is particularly interested or absorbed by certain parts or aspects. Other parts or aspects may go by unnoticed altogether. And so it is possible that two critics can argue about a film (from opposite points of view) and yet both be right, because they are not really discussing one film, but *two* films—the two subjective streams they separately experienced.

How, then, are we ever to hope to understand one another? Is there any more objective basis of criticism? Can we establish some sort of criterion which will take into account the limitations of our own perceptions as well as those of others? Yes, I think so, if we learn something of how we make judgments from moment to moment in everyday experience.

Very few of us have any idea how we do in fact arrive at judgments. We think them very simple. We take them for granted. Actually, they are not simple, but complex. What seems to us to be one single, simple judgment is really a composite of reactions from different parts of ourselves. These various component parts may be harmonious, but more often than not they are unrelated, or even contradictory.

In everyone, it seems, there are three chief functioning parts, each with its own kind of experience, reactions, and form of judgment.

1. *The physical apparatus* that deals with instinctive and motor sensations: sight, sound, taste, smell, touch, heat, cold, pressure, balance, pain, etc. All our movements are governed by this apparatus. Through it we judge where we should run to catch a thrown ball, or how to balance on one foot. We clearly do not make these judgments through our emotions or our intellect.

2. *The emotional apparatus.* Our likes and dislikes. Pleasant emotions, such as joy, humor, love, courage. Unpleasant emotions, such as hate, fear, depression, anger. Emotional judgments are irrational—often conflicting with those of the intellect and the motor mechanism; fear can make it impossible for us to walk a plank one foot wide, sixty feet in the air, although we are physically capable of it.

3. *The intellectual apparatus.* This works with thoughts and ideas. It is unemotional, but can think about and compare the results of various emotions. It makes patterns, real or imaginary; works out formulae, laws, etc. It makes judgments on the relative values of different sensations, emotions, and ideas.

All of us, of course, have all three of these apparatuses. And each of them properly should provide us independently with a different aspect of the whole truth about any experience. The trouble is that practically none of us—neither artist, nor onlooker—has a natural balance of the three functions. In each of us, one of them tends to predominate to the extent of weakening the other two, or preventing their development. The predominant function is also the most comfortable one, and we rely on it more and more, until finally it tends to govern the whole of our lives, instead of only a third of it. . . .

In sum, each of our functions makes its own separate judgment on what is being placed before it. We can be intellectually convinced without being emotionally convinced—and so on for all the possible combinations. Unless all three parts of us are simultaneously convinced, it is not a complete conviction. . . . In the creative work of the artist, all three functions play their separate parts. If they go deep and work together harmoniously, we have "inspired" art, in which the meaning and intensity of emotion are one with the physical embodiment or rendering. On the other hand, if any of the artist's functions are underdeveloped, warped, or out of balance, the work of art suffers the corresponding imperfections.

But the *experience* of the work of art is incomplete until we add to all this the perception of the viewer or critic. Objective criticism **requires** that the critic understand his own psychological make-up, as well as the artist's. The critic can only appreciate a work of art to the extent that his own perceptions are sensitive, developed, and harmonized. If a work of art does not arouse or please him, it may be due to the imperfections of the artist, or of the execution of the work itself; but it may also be due to his own lacks, limitations and imbalances. This, too, is part of the material to be criticized. And the hopeful thing is that it is possible for us to extend our own capacity to perceive and to criticize effectively, by discovering which of our functions are least developed and learning how to balance them up and make them work together. Too often our role in the audience is an automatic, passive one. It ought to be, and *can* be, an active, creative one.

Charlie Chaplin

The George Jean Nathan quotation is from *Art of the Night* (New York: Knopf, 1928), in the chapter entitled "Notes on the Movies," which contains some brilliant, and some odd, observations and comments.

The quotations from Chaplin himself appeared in an article entitled "Incunabula Cinematographica," by R. K. Neilson Baxter, in *The Cinema 1950* (Harmondsworth, England: Pelican, 1950), edited by Roger Manvell; they were taken in turn from Louis Delluc's 1922 book on Chaplin, and portions reappear in Chaplin's *Autobiography* (New York: Simon and Schuster, 1964) and were reprinted in Harry M. Geduld's anthology, *Film Makers on Film Making* (Bloomington and London: Indiana University Press, 1967).

Henry O'Higgins' review of *The Pawnshop* appeared in the February 3, 1917, issue of *The New Republic*. A detailed description of the same film, using longer words, is included as an appendix to Gilbert Seldes' *The Seven Lively Arts* (New York: Harper, 1924).

Theodore Huff's *Charlie Chaplin* (New York: Henry Schuman, 1951) is the most readable and informative book about Chaplin and his films. *The Films of Charlie Chaplin*, edited by Gerald McDonald, Michael Conway, and Mark Ricci (New York: Citadel, 1965) contains a sketchy synopsis of each film, shorts as well as features, with excerpts of reviews printed at the time of release.

William Faulkner's formula for success appeared in *Writers at Work* (New York: Viking, 1959), a collection of interviews from *The Paris Review*, edited by Malcolm Cowley. The Faulkner interview also includes comments about his experiences as a Hollywood scriptwriter.

Films: All the Mutual comedies (1916-17) are available for 16mm, 8mm, and Super-8 purchase from Blackhawk Films, 1235 West Fifth Street, Davenport, Iowa 52808. They are also available for 16mm rental from other commercial distributors (Contemporary/McGraw-Hill Films and CCM Films have prints with added music and sound effects—which I do not favor; Film Images circulates four films on a program, which is entirely too much at one time).

Following are the titles I recommend most highly: *The Pawnshop, The Cure, The Immigrant*—all **** films; and *The Adventurer, The Rink, Easy Street, One A.M., The Floorwalker* (all ***).

Chaplin's earlier Keystone and Essanay shorts are also available from Blackhawk and other sources and can be sampled judiciously to show the rapid development of Chaplin's style. In selecting titles, it may be a good idea to read the descriptions in the Huff book, or in the book by McDonald, Conway, and Ricci, to find subjects that seem most appropriate to your age-group.

Projects: It is interesting to compare Chaplin's style—especially his pretended transformations—with that of other outstanding movie comedians. I recommend Buster Keaton's *Cops* (1922), *The Balloonatic* (1923), and *One Week* (1921)—along with *Sherlock Jr.* (1924), which contains one of the world's funniest parodies on film editing. The first three are each about 20 minutes long, and the last runs about 50 minutes. All can be rented from CCM Films, 866 Third Avenue, New York, New York 10022. *The Balloonatic* and *Cops* are also available for 16mm, 8mm, and Super-8 purchase from Blackhawk Films.

Note: I have shown Chaplin's short films, mainly the Mutual films, to nearly every class I've taught—which, if we include the massive program that went into the auditoriums of some 100 high schools and junior high schools in New York State, would total about 75,000 students. The great majority knew immediately that Chaplin was in a class by himself; a few thought him funny, but not unusually so; a very small number found him uninteresting, or even unpleasant. Compare this average to the election of a very popular President, when 55 percent of the voters is considered a sign of tremendous popularity.

It is unfortunate that some students are afraid to laugh at the films, or to write that they liked the films—because school has never encouraged the sense of fun. One student expressed his ambivalent feelings in this way:

My impression of Charlie Chaplin's movie was it was rediculas! It was pretty funny in places, but still rediculas. I thought it was one of the worst I ever saw. But I liked it anyway.

With all the problems that must be faced in schools today, a little laughter can hardly be a dangerous thing.

The Chaplin shorts are occasionally run on television, which loses many of his gestures with hand and feet due to picture reduction on all four sides of the image. Chaplin put movement into the entire picture area, not merely into the central portion where most filmmakers concentrate their attention.

"I am surprised that some critics say that my camera technique is old-fashioned, that I have not kept up with the times. What times? My technique is the outgrowth of thinking for myself, of my own logic and approach; it is not borrowed from what others are doing."

—Chaplin, in *My Autobiography*

Robert Flaherty and *Nanook of the North*

Robert Flaherty wrote and told many versions of how his first film was made. "How I Filmed *Nanook of the North* is included in Harry M. Geduld's anthology, *Film Makers on Film Making*, and "Robert Flaherty Talking" is included in *The Cinema 1950.*

Flaherty's marvelous book entitled *My Eskimo Friends* (New York: Doubleday, Page, 1924) tells of his northern expeditions; it is the basis for much of the Eskimo sections in Richard Griffith's *The World of Robert Flaherty* (New York: Duell Sloan & Pearce, 1953) and Arthur Calder-Marshall's *The Innocent Eye: The Life of Robert J. Flaherty* (London: W. H. Allen, 1963).

George C. Pratt's two-volume spiral-bound *Spellbound in Darkness* (Rochester: University School, 1966), an annotated selection of readings about the silent film, contains Frances Taylor Patterson's fine review of *Nanook*, which appeared in the August 9, 1922, issue of *The New Republic*. In it she wrote that the film "marks the beginning of the naturalistic school of cinematography . . . achieved through the purely artificial means of the camera."

In the same anthology, *Spellbound in Darkness*, there is Mrs. Robert Flaherty's article entitled "The Camera Eye" (reprinted from *The National Board of Review Magazine*, April 1927), in which she wrote about the camera's uncanny ability to see and record more than the human eye can see.

Films: Ninety Degrees South, running 75-minutes, with a soundtrack that was added in 1933, is available for rental only to educational groups from the Museum of Modern Art Film Library, 11 West 53rd Street, New York, New York 10019. (*Scott's Last Journey*, a recent one-hour BBC-TV production, uses some of the Ponting footage and still photographs but lacks the vitality of the original film; distributed for 16mm rental and purchase from Contemporary/McGraw-Hill, 330 West 42nd Street, New York, New York 10036.)

Nanook of the North is available in the original silent version from the Museum of Modern Art Film Library. A silent version with music track added is available from Contemporary/McGraw-Hill.

An excellent contrast with *Nanook* is found in the film entitled *Grass*, made in 1925 by Meriam C. Cooper and Ernest B. Schoedsack (who later achieved screen immortality with their production of *King Kong*). The film records the migration of some 50,000 Bakhtiari nomads, with their sheep, cattle, and household goods, in search of pasture lands. A forty-minute condensation of the seven-reel feature film includes the two most spectacular sequences: crossing the icy river on home-made pontoons, and climbing the snow-clad mountains barefooted. But because we see no close and intimate scenes of the chief and his son, as we do with Nanook and his family, we remain observers of the incredible spectacle, rather than participants. The short version of *Grass* is available for 16mm rental from Film Classic Exchange, 1926 South Vermont Avenue, Los Angeles, California 90007.

Although all the above films are longer than desirable for the average 45-minute class period, they can be broken down into several parts for classroom presentation. (They are also fine for auditorium showing, in which case it is usually helpful to give a very brief introduction mentioning several sequences of particular interest.)

After showing the igloo sequence of *Nanook*, you may find it interesting to screen the Canadian Film Board's *How to Build an Igloo* (11 minutes, color), available for 16mm rental and purchase from Sterling Films, 241 East 24th Street, New York, New York 10016. While the latter is well made, with all the essential details clearly shown, it lacks the "little touches" of personal involvement that make Flaherty's sequence unforgettable.

A Personal Note on Robert Flaherty

I met Flaherty several times, early in my documentary film reviewing career, and one of those occasions has recurred many times in my memory. I was late arriving at a preview of some European art films. The program had started, and most of the seats were filled. An empty seat was pointed out to me, in the middle of a row, and I shuffled across feet and knees to get to it. Scarcely had I sat down when the man at my right tugged at my elbow and began whispering into my ear, in a very loud voice. "Good heavens," I told myself, "not only am I late, not only have I stepped on people's toes, but I'm obviously sitting in a seat that was intended for someone else."

I looked over to see who was pulling at my elbow, and even in the semi-dark the face was easily recognizable. It was Robert Flaherty. What will I say when the lights go on between films, I wondered. What will he say when he sees that I'm not the person he was expecting?

When the lights went on, he went right on talking to me, as if I were the very person he was expecting, indeed the only person who might possibly have been expected. We had talked at a film meeting a year or so before, but he could not possibly have had any idea who I was or what I did. None of that mattered to Flaherty. His great gift of relating wholeheartedly to whoever was there is of course evident in all his films.

I saw another special gift that Flaherty possessed as the evening went on. Some of the films we saw were dull, but occasionally there were moments of beauty or of some excitement. Flaherty seemed often to doze through the bad parts, but as soon as something began to happen on the screen, he was wide-awake, likely as not tugging at my elbow again, commenting on the loveliness or strangeness there before us. To tune out the things that are of little value, and to tune in on those that are, is a rare talent we might all try to cultivate. **139**

From Abstract to Concrete

The Richter quotation at the opening of the chapter is from an interview published in *Film Culture*, Winter 1963-64. The quotations about *Ghosts Before Breakfast* appear in the booklet, *Hans Richter, Painting and Film* (1970), published in connection with an exhibition at the Goethe-Institute in Munich. Richter's "Avant-Garde Film in Germany" appears in *Experiment in the Film*, edited by Roger Manvell, and his "History of the Avant-garde" is included in *Art in Cinema*, edited by Frank Stauffacher (both books have been reprinted by the Arno Press/New York Times, 1970).

Hans Richter by Hans Richter, edited by Cleve Gray (New York: Holt, Rinehart and Winston, 1971) is a marvelously illustrated volume of Richter's life and work in film and various art media, written in the artist's own words.

The lengthy quotation about the filming of *Rain* is from Joris Ivens' *The Camera and I* (New York: International Publishers, 1969).

Films: Richter on Film (15 minutes, color), produced especially for use with this book, is a resumé of Richter's career as an artist and filmmaker, including excerpts from the short films he discusses. It is available for 16mm rental and purchase from Star Films, Department 8A, 50 West 96th Street, New York, New York 10025. *Ghosts Before Breakfast*, and a combination reel of Viking Eggeling's *Symphonie Diagonale* and Richter's *Rhythmus 21*—the first abstract films ever made—are also distributed by Star Films for 16mm rental and purchase.

Anaemic Cinema, Rain, and *H_2O* can be rented on 16mm from the Museum of Modern Art Film Library, 11 West 53rd Street, New York, New York, 10019, to educational groups only.

The Ruttmann abstract films are not circulated in this country, to my knowledge.

Projects: Art students should be able to design their own turntable movies, for use on any ordinary phonograph. To get a sense of the motion and dimension in Duchamp's designs, hold the picture on page 71 with both hands and tilt it from one side to another as rapidly as possible.

From Silence to Sound

The chapter entitled "The Movies Learn to Talk," in Arthur Knight's *The Liveliest Art* (New York: Macmillan, 1957) opens with ten pages that are pertinent to this study.

Films: The Movies March On (1939, 22 minutes), a March of Time episode about film history from the beginning to 1939, shows some of the ways in which sound affected films; it is available for 16mm rental to educational groups only from the Museum of Modern Art Film Library, 11 West 53rd Street, New York, New York 10019.

The Movies Learn to Talk (1963, 27 minutes), originally produced for the CBS-TV series, "Twentieth Century," is an entertaining glimpse into the science and art of sound in films, emphasizing pre-1927 experiments; it is available for 16mm rental and purchase from McGraw-Hill Text-Films, 330 West 42nd Street, New York, New York 10036.

Let's Go to the Movies and *The Soundman* (each 8 minutes) are promotional Hollywood films, made in 1951, each of which has some interesting footage. The former includes an unidentified glimpse of Méliès taking off his head, the scene atop the moving train in *The Great Train Robbery*, Al Jolson in blackface as *The Jazz Singer*, and John Barrymore in whiteface as Don Juan. *The Soundman* shows how dialogue is recorded and mixed with music and sound effect tracks to make the finished soundtrack—along with excerpts from early sound films. Prints are available for five-year lease at a price only slightly higher than cost from Teaching Film Custodians, 25 West 45th Street, New York, New York 10036, and for rental from a number of university film libraries. They are circulated to schools only.

Grierson and the Documentary Movement

Arthur Knight's *The Liveliest Art* has an interesting twelve pages on "England and the Documentary Tradition." Edgar Anstey's "Development of Film Technique in Britain," included in *Experiment in the Film*, edited by Roger Manvell (and reprinted by The Arno Press/New York Times, 1970) has first-hand information about the documentary movement.

Grierson on Documentary (Berkeley: University of California Press, 1966), edited by Forsyth Hardy, is somewhat advanced for an introductory study of film, but it can be sampled judiciously for an appreciation of Grierson's astute mind and his great love of the movies.

The Technique of Film Editing (New York: Hastings House, 1968), written and compiled by Karel Reisz and Gavin Millar for the British Film Academy, is an enlarged edition of Reisz's 1953 work, with a lengthy analysis of sounds and shots in *Night Mail* and several pages on *Song of Ceylon*. Ernest Lindgren's *The Art of the Film* (New York: Macmillan, 1970) contains the entire Auden poem from *Night Mail* and comments on its use within the film.

Films: Granton Trawler is available for 16mm rental and purchase, and *Night Mail* for 16mm rental only, from Contemporary/McGraw-Hill, 330 West 42nd Street, New York, New York 10036. Both are available for 16mm rental only to educational groups from the Museum of Modern Art Film Library, 11 West 53rd Street, New York, New York 10019.

Song of Ceylon, Housing Problems, Listen to Britain, And So They Live, Valley Town, and *The River* are also available for 16mm rental from the Museum of Modern Art Film Library. *And So They Live* and *Valley Town* are available for 16mm rental and purchase from the New York University Film Library, 26 Washington Place, New York, New York 10003. *The River* is available for 16mm purchase, at slightly above print cost, from Du Art Film Laboratories, Inc., U.S. Government Films, 245 West 55th Street, New York, New York 10019, and for 16mm rental from almost every film library.

These six documentary films date from the 1930s and '40s and are valuable as important historical documents as well as classics of the motion picture. Teachers who wish to use them with beginning film students should help recreate the period from which they emerge and the social questions with which they deal. For this they may require the background of a social studies or history expert.

Reality and the Story Film

The John Gould Fletcher quotation is from his excellent essay, *The Crisis of the Film* (Seattle: University of Washington, 1929; reprinted in *Screen Monographs II*, New York: Arno Press/New York Times, 1970.)

Lewis Jacobs' quotation about *The Bridge* is in the essay, "Experimental Cinema in America 1921-1947," in the 1968 edition of *The Rise of the American Film* (New York: Teachers College, 1968), which also appears in Roger Manvell's anthology, *Experiment in The Film* (reprinted by The Arno Press/New York Times, 1970).

Films: The Critic and 'The Overlanders' is available for 16mm rental from Contemporary/McGraw-Hill, 330 West 42nd Street, New York, New York 10036. Educational organizations may obtain long-lease prints of this and other films in this series from the British Film Institute, 81, Dean Street, London, W. IV 6AA, England.

You Can't Run Away, excerpted from MGM's *Intruder in the Dust*, can be leased by schools and colleges for five years from Teaching Film Custodians, 25 West 45th Street, New York, New York 10036, and can be rented from a number of TFC depository film libraries. (Note: While most of the TFC films are chosen for literary or historical subject matter, rather than significance in their own artistic right, a few are fine examples of the best Hollywood styles. Others I have used and can recommend are: *Due Process of Law Denied*, a 29-minute excerpt from *The Ox-Bow Incident* (1942) and *Some People Stayed Home*, 9 minutes from Preston Sturges' *The Great McGinty* (1942.)

The American Film is available on 16mm for five-year lease from Teaching Film Custodians, to schools and colleges only. I realize that it is not fair to criticize sequences from long films isolated from the rest of the film. Generally they give no sense of the thread of action and the emotional excitement that sustains the film. Still, in my experience, it is only by studying one or two sequences of a feature film that we can begin to understand the strengths and weaknesses of its general style.

An Occurrence at Owl Creek Bridge is available for 16mm rental and purchase from Contemporary/McGraw-Hill, 330 West 42nd Street, New York, New York 10036; it is included in almost every educational film library in the country. (The Bierce story can be found in many anthologies, and can be used for discussion and for script-writing practice with students who can work on so advanced a level.)

The Bridge (sometimes called *The Spy*) is available for 16mm rental from CCM Films, 866 Third Avenue, New York, New York 10022.

The student production of *An Occurrence at Owl Creek Bridge*, in color, is available for 16mm rental and purchase from the University of Southern California, Division of Cinema, Film Distribution Section, University Park, Los Angeles, California 90007.

The Art of Animation

Oskar Fischinger: An almost complete selection of Fischinger's films is available for 16mm rental and purchase from the Los Angeles Filmmakers Cooperative, 8925 Wonderland Park Avenue, Hollywood, California 90046—and from Pyramid Films, Box 1048, Santa Monica, California 90406.

The Museum of Modern Art Film Library, 11 West 53rd Street, New York, New York 10019, has a 13-minute reel containing four of the black-and-white Film Studies (Nos. 6, 7, 8, and 11), an 11-minute color reel containing *Composition in Blue, Circle, Allegretto*, and *An American March*, and the 10-minute color film entitled *Motion Painting No. 1*. The reels are available for 16mm rental to educational groups only; if you rent either of the first two reels, show no more than two of the short films at one sitting.

Oskar Fischinger's "My Statements are in My Work" is included in *Art in Cinema*, edited by Frank Stauffacher (San Francisco Museum of Art, 1947, reprinted by Arno Press/New York Times, 1970). McLaren's statement about first seeing a Fischinger film is from "Talking to a Great Film Artist: Norman McLaren Interviewed by Don McWilliams," in the April 28, 1969, issue of *The McGill Reporter*. The Lewis Jacobs quotation is from his essay "Experimental Cinema in America 1921-47," included in the new edition of *The Rise of the American Film* (New York: Teachers College, 1968), and in the Arno Press/New York Times 1970 reprint of Roger Manvell's *Experiment in the Film*.

Len Lye: The McLaren quotations are from a letter written to the author, August 18, 1952. The color process used by Len Lye, or one of the processes, is described on pp. 87-8 of *The Technique of Film Animation* (New York: Hastings House, 1968) by John Halas and Roger Manvell. The statements by Len Lye about sponsored films are from his reply to a questionnaire sent out by the author in the winter of 1957.

The remaining quotations from Len Lye are from an interview with Gretchen Weinberg, in the Summer 1963 issue of *Film Culture* (#29). The Mancia-Van Dyke quotation is from "The Artist as Film-Maker: Len Lye," in the July-August 1966 issue of *Art in America*.

The early Len Lye films are available individually for 16mm rental to educational groups only from the Museum of Modern Art Film Library, 11 West 53rd Street, New York, New York 10019. Titles are *A Color Box, Trade Tattoo, Musical Poster No. One*, and *Swinging the Lambeth Walk*. (*Rainbow Dance* has been withdrawn, but it is so spectacular a film that every effort should be made to put it back in circulation—even in the limited circulation of the Museum of Modern Art.)

Carmen D'Avino: Jonas Mekas's comments about the D'Avino films appeared in the April 20, 1967, issue of *The Village Voice*, in his weekly film column. D'Avino's comments on his techniques and aims are based on a cable-TV interview with the author in the spring of 1969.

The D'Avino films are available for 16mm rental and purchase from Grove Press Films, 53 East 11th Street, New York, New York 10003. (Several of the very short films are grouped three or four to a reel, but they can also be rented or purchased individually if you so specify).

Alexander Alexeieff: The quotation that opens this chapter is from "The Fleeting Art," by Alexander Alexeieff, in the Winter 1965-66 issue of the *Cinema TV Digest* (Vol. 4, No. 1). Other Alexeieff quotations are from his "Reflections on Motion Picture Animation," in the Spring 1964 issue of *Film Culture* (No. 32). Additional information has been received from letters and personal conversations.

McLaren's comments about *Night on Bald Mountain* are from the program of the Oxford Animation Festival, published in London in 1970. Alexeieff's detailed description of the Pinboard and his "illusory solids" can be found on pp. 304-5 of Halas and Manvell's *The Technique of Film Animation* (New York: Hastings House, 1968).

The films, *Night on Bald Mountain, The Nose*, and *Alexeieff at the Pinboard*, are available for 16mm rental and purchase from Star Films, Department 8A, 50 West 96th Street, New York, New York 10025. The reel of color commercials is available for 16mm rental only, from Star Films, at the same address.

Class Projects: After screening *The Nose*, try another Gogol story turned into a film, entitled *The Bespoke Overcoat* (37 minutes), it was produced in 1955, directed by Jack Clayton, photographed by Wolf Suschitzky, and features the actors David Kossoff and Alfie Bass. Scriptwriter Wolf Mankowitz has changed the locale from Russia to London's ghetto district at the turn of the century and has given story precedence over fantasy. Some students may enjoy comparing *The Nose* and *The Bespoke Overcoat* to the stories from which they were adapted, and to each other. *The Bespoke Overcoat* is available for 16mm rental and purchase from Encyclopaedia Britannica Education Corporation, 425 North Michigan Avenue, Chicago, Illinois 60611.

The paperback *Animation in the Cinema* (New York: A. S. Barnes, 1967), by Ralph Stevenson, has bits about almost every animator in the world, including Fischinger (pp. 64-5), Len Lye (pp. 79-80) and Alexeieff (pp. 93-5); the book is recommended mainly for its low cost and its pleasant illustrations.

Norman McLaren and the Essence of Animation

The quotation that opens the McLaren chapter is from an article by Ernest Callenbach in the Winter 1962-63 issue of *Film Quarterly*. McLaren's comments about low budgets are from an interview by Forsyth Hardy, broadcast on the Scottish Home Service of the BBC on November 22, 1951. The comments about making *Blinkity Blank* are from a promotion flyer printed by the National Film Board of Canada.

The National Film Board has also published McLaren's technical notes explaining how each of his films was made, in reasonable detail. Film teachers may write for these, specifying the film or films they are most interested in, to the Animation Department, National Film Board of Canada, P. O. Box 6100, Montreal 101, Quebec, Canada.

In the following articles, available without charge while they last, McLaren discusses his techniques and materials so that anyone who wishes may try them or create his own versions. The secret, you will soon discover, is not in the *technique* but in the *doing*.

"Cameraless Animation: A Technique Developed at the National Film Board of Canada," by Norman McLaren, 11 pp.: an illustrated step-by-step guide, specific, direct, delightful, and—believe it or not—written in 1949, when today's film teachers were still children and today's film students were not yet born!

"Talking to a Great Film Artist: Norman McLaren Interviewed by Don McWilliams," a large four-page newspaper reprint, with many illustrations, plus considerable information about the making of *Pas de Deux*. (Reprinted from the April 28, 1969, issue of *The McGill Reporter*).

"The Unique Genius of Norman McLaren," by May Ebbitt Cutler (reprinted from *Canadian Art*, May/June 1965), 10 pp., with many illustrations, some in color.

The above pamphlets are available from the National Film Board of Canada, 680 Fifth Avenue, New York, New York 10019 —and some are also available from the International Film Bureau, 332 South Michigan Avenue, Chicago, Illinois 60604.

Films: All the McLaren films are available for 16mm rental and purchase from the International Film Bureau and from Pyramid Films, Box 1048, Santa Monica, California 90406. Most of the titles can be rented from Contemporary/McGraw-Hill, 330 West 42nd Street, New York, New York 10036. *Pas de Deux* and *The Eye Hears, The Ear Speaks* can also be rented or purchased from the Learning Corporation of America, 711 Fifth Avenue, New York, New York 10022.

There are about two dozen McLaren films to choose from, every one of which is a delightful surprise, but for beginning students I most heartedly recommend *Fiddle-de-dee, Hen Hop, Le Merle, Two Bagatelles* and *Pen Point Percussion* and *Loops.* After that, you must screen *Neighbors, Pas de Deux, Rhythmetic, Stars and Stripes, A Chairy Tale, Blinkity Blank,* and on, and on. The more often you see them, the more fun they are—except for *Neighbors,* which is a memorable, but devastating, experience.

Fantasy and Reality: A Conclusion

The Richter quotation at the end of the chapter is from a booklet published by the Finch College Art Museum. The comments on *Highway* are from a classroom test paper written by Suzanne K. Leonard, when she was in the eighth grade.

Films: In the Street is available for 16mm rental from the Museum of Modern Art Film Library, 11 West 53rd Street, New York, New York 10019, to educational groups only.

The films of Hilary Harris—*Generation, Longhorns,* and *Highway*—are available for 16mm rental and purchase from Film Images, 17 West 60th Street, New York, New York 10023.

The Canaries is available for 16mm rental and purchase from Noel Productions, 1860 Broadway, New York, New York 10023.

N.Y., N.Y. is available for 16mm rental and purchase from Pyramid Films, Box 1048, Santa Monica, California 90406, and for 16mm rental, to educational groups only, from the Museum of Modern Art Film Library.

Daybreak Express is available for 16mm rental and purchase from Pennebaker Productions, 56 West 45th Street, New York, New York 10036.

Class Projects: The similarities and differences between *N.Y., N.Y.* and *Daybreak Express* provide good material for class analysis. Both Francis Thompson and Donn Pennebaker are expert technicians, with fine eyes for pattern, movement, and color.

Both are established filmmakers, in quite different styles. Thompson specializes in extravagant multiscreen presentations, such as the popular *To Be Alive!* made in collaboration with Alexander Hammid for the 1964-5 New York World's Fair. Pennebaker specializes in *cinema-vérité,* the unscripted filming of real events and personalities, such as the features *Monterey Pop* and Bob Dylan's *Don't Look Back.* Before either was established independently, they worked on many short documentary films produced by the pioneer educational filmmaker, Julien Bryan.

How we react to these two films is largely a matter of taste. I like both films, but for different reasons. In *Daybreak Express* I like the brevity (five minutes seems ample for this eye-popping kind of photography), the music (the rhythmic beat helps keep the images moving), and the continuity (from everyday reality to various kinds of fantasy, then back again to reality). In *N.Y., N.Y.* I like the playful humor (trick shots of feet walking down the street with other feet on top of them); the Daliesque oozings of the images (liquid buses and taxicabs); the rich display of color (dull, bright, gaudy, all rather synthetic-looking).

Students may discuss other things they liked or didn't like in these two films—and may also talk about the difficulties that confront our eyes and minds when we look at unusual or unexpected images in a film.

In this connection, it might be helpful to review such articles as H. F. Hoffman's "Cutting Off the Feet," which first appeared in the April 6, 1912, issue of *The Moving Picture World* (and is reprinted in George C. Pratt's *Spellbound in Darkness,* published by the University of Rochester, 1966). Hoffman argued against the growing tendency to cut off the actors' feet in many movies of the time, and the worse practice of cutting off the figures at the knees. The article concluded: "A picture is a combination of several factors into a complete and harmonious whole. An arrangement with the feet cut off is not a complete and harmonious whole. There is something lacking." Mr. Hoffman is indeed correct. Something is lacking when the feet are cut off. But it is also correct to say that something else is added. When unusual techniques are used in a film, we should try to assess the gain as well as the loss, if we are to keep discovering more and more about the movies.

Note on the Availability of Film Books:

Most of the books mentioned above are available in both hardcover and paperback editions. If you have difficulty locating any of them, or if you wish to place a large order, it may be quickest and easiest to order from a book shop that specializes in film. Their prices for out-of-print books range from moderate to very high; some put out regular catalogues, so shop around for the best buys, if you have the time.

Notes on the Availability of Films:

As the final material for this book was being typed, I received word that the Museum of Modern Art Film Library has re-released the full-length 64-minute version of *Grass* (1925), which was out of circulation for several years. It is typical of nontheatrical film distribution that films go in and out of circulation without warning and that they pass from one distributor's hands to another's, at seven-year intervals (the usual length of a distribution contract).

It is inevitable, then, that the information details given in this book will become more and more out-of-date. However, if you send for distributors' free catalogues, get on their mailing lists, and use the libraries closest to you for rentals, you should be able to keep up with most of the changes. (It is also not too much to expect a distributor to notify you of a change in distribution arrangements of the film you want, or even to send the request on to the new distributor!)

A selection of the films described in **Discovering the Movies** has been brought together for convenient 16mm rental and purchase by the publisher. For an up-to-date listing of titles and prices, write VNR Films, Van Nostrand Reinhold Company, 450 West 33rd Street, New York, New York 10001.

Acknowledgments:

The following people have been particularly helpful to me during the years in which the material for this book was being developed:

Ronald Mace, who was determined that I should have a chance to teach film to his eighth and ninth grade students.

Many former students who were helpful in special ways, particularly James Watters, Roger Sandall, Merle Worth, Gary Carey, Gordon Hitchens, John Gatto, Sheryl Starke, Suzanne Leonard, and the several hundred others who helped me learn with them.

Marcia Clark, George Teter, Elizabeth White, Sue Burchard, and Laura Hudley, who have given their opinions and suggestions about the lay-out and content of this book, and who have participated with me in forming the West Side Film Teachers Co-op.

Eileen Bowser, Guy Glover, Frances Flaherty, Blanche Sweet, and others who read certain chapters of the manuscript and made suggestions for their improvement.

Susan Baris Mace, who has put many of my film teaching ideas into practice and improved upon many others, and who gave invaluable suggestions on the re-writing of early drafts of the manuscript.

Grace George Alexander, whose alertness and concern brought author and publisher together at the very right moment.

I wish also to thank the film distributors who have kindly made their films available for re-screening as needed: Kent D. Eastin, of Blackhawk Films; Leo Dratfield, Nancy O'Rourke and Ann Schutzer, of Contemporary /McGraw-Hill; Peggy Kenas, of Film Bureau; Rosalind Kossoff, formerly of Film Images, and Carolyn Henig, currently of Film Images; Kenneth Shere of the Canadian National Film Board's New York office; Stanley McIntosh, of Teaching Film Custodians; Myron Bresnick, of Audio Films (now CCM); and Charles M. Tarbox, of Film Classic Exchange.

Thanks are due Tom C. Daly, of the National Film Board of Canada, for permission to reprint "The Audience is Part of the Film."

Some of the material in this book has been re-written from earlier articles and reviews first published in *The Saturday Review, House Beautiful, The EFLA Bulletin, Film News,* and *Popular Photography,* and is included here by permission of the publishers.

Small grants, amounting to one or two hundred dollars a year, were made available to the author for 16mm film rentals, from the New York State Council on the Arts, Peter Bradley and Barbara Haspiel in charge of film activities.

I am deeply indebted to Jean Koefoed, for allowing this book to be arranged according to my general plan.

Picture Credits

The following filmmakers kindly supplied still pictures of themselves and/ or their films: Alexander Alexeieff and Claire Parker, Carmen D'Avino, Hilary Harris, Jerome Hill, Roger Leenhardt, Helen Levitt, Donn Pennebaker, Hans Richter, and Francis Thompson. I am indebted also to Mrs. Elfriede Fischinger for photographs and other material concerning Oskar Fischinger; to Mme. Madeleine Malthête-Méliès and Maxine Haleff, for pictures of Georges Méliès and scenes from some of his films; and to Vachel Lindsay Blair, for the photograph of his uncle, Vachel Lindsay.

Many of the Flaherty stills in this book are from the Flaherty Collection, now being catalogued at the School of Theology in Claremont, California, under the direction of W. Jack Coogan. I am deeply grateful to Mrs. Frances Flaherty for permission to use them.

The National Film Board of Canada supplied an abundance of material on the films of Norman McLaren, and McLaren himself was thoughtful enough to send me some of his original hand-colored film frames to be photographed for inclusion in this book.

Special thanks are due Kent D. Eastin, president of Blackhawk Films, who supplied many stills, and allowed other stills to be made up from 16mm prints of the films in his distribution library.

Forsyth Hardy was kind enough to rush a selection of stills from the Edinburgh Film Guild from *Nanook of the North, Granton Trawler, Night Mail, Housing Problems,* and *Song of Ceylon.*

I am also indebted to Janus Films for the photograph of Ingmar Bergman; to the Eastman Kodak Company for the pictures of the film strips; to the Milton Bradley Company for the photograph of the old Zoetrope; to the George Eastman House for pictures of the Praxinoscope, Muybridge's race track, and his running horses; to the Netherlands Film Museum for stills from Joris Ivens' *Rain;* to Contemporary-McGraw-Hill for stills from *An Occurrence at Owl Creek Bridge* and two stills from *Nanook of the North;* to the Learning Corporation of America for one of the stills from *Pas de Deux.*

Stills from the following feature films are reproduced by permission of their distributors: United Artists (*Red River, The Horse Soldiers, High Noon*), Paramount (*Shane*), Columbia (*On the Waterfront*), and Allied Artists (*Friendly Persuasion*). These stills are copyrighted. All rights reserved.

The Museum of Modern Art Stills Library supplied pictures from *Workers Leaving the Lumière Factory* and the Lumière poster; *A Trip to the Moon, The Conquest of the Pole,* and Méliès' studio; *The Great Train Robbery,* Edwin S. Porter, and *Rescued from an Eagle's Nest;* D. W. Griffith, *The Lonedale Operator, The New York Hat,* the United Artists group; *The Devil's Wanton;* Chaplin; *Ninety Degrees South; Nanook of the North; Anaemic Cinema, Rain,* and *H₂O; The Jazz Singer; Granton Trawler, Night Mail,* and *The Overlanders;* Len Lye, *Trade Tattoo* and *Free Radicals.*

Other stills were obtained from the New York Public Library, Cinemabilia, Anthology Film Archives, and from several private collections, including that of the author.

Index